**THE AMEN CORNER · BLUES FOR MISTER CHARLIE
ONE DAY, WHEN I WAS LOST**
Distinguished Laurel Editions of the Plays of

JAMES BALDWIN

James Baldwin

one day, when I was lost

**a scenario based on Alex Haley's
"The Autobiography of Malcolm X"**

A LAUREL BOOK
Published by
Dell Publishing
a division of
Bantam Doubleday Dell Publishing Group, Inc.
666 Fifth Avenue
New York, New York 10103

ISBN: 0-440-20660-X

Printed in the United States of America
Published simultaneously in Canada

March 1990

10 9 8 7 6 5 4 3 2 1

KRI

(The late afternoon, in New York, from the Statue of Liberty in the bay, and the busy water traffic, the downtown spires, the midtown spires, then the garage of the New York Hilton Hotel.

The garage is utterly silent, long and ominous.

The door leading to the hotel opens, and a man's long, lean silhouette crosses the garage swiftly and gets into a car.

There is a long pause before he turns on the ignition and the sound of the motor rolls through the garage.

The moment we hear the sound of the motor, the car's side-view mirror fills the screen—as blank as the garage. The radio begins to play—"soul" music—and the car's side-view mirror begins to move, up, into the daylight.

We see the driver's bespectacled eyes in the rear-view mirror: eyes both haunted and alert.

The music pauses. We hear an announcement that MALCOLM X will be appearing at the Audubon Ballroom in the evening.

The side-view mirror, reflecting darkness, then light, then the traffic in the streets.

A red light; people crossing the street; soul music.

We now see the driver, MALCOLM X, bearded, harried, and yet, at the same time, calm and proud.

As the car begins to move again, the side-view mirror begins to reflect inexplicable images, swift, overlapping, blurred.

A fire fills the screen. Then, hooded men, on horseback, smashing in the windows of a country house; a fair, young mulatto woman, pregnant, flinching as the horsemen ride between her and the house; and between her and the camera.

A voice is heard, shouting, "Brothers, sisters, this is not our home! Our homeland is in Africa! *In Africa!*"

We hear a trolley-car's clanging bell, and see, from the point of view of the motorman, a beaten, one-eyed black man, lying across the streetcar tracks, watching his death approach.

MALCOLM's face.

The car is moving uptown, through the streets of Manhattan, and we watch MALCOLM watching the people and watching the tall, proud buildings. Following MALCOLM's eye, we begin picking out, isolating, certain details of these buildings:

A cupola, at the topmost height of a New York building, transforms itself, as we pass, into the balcony of the presidential mansion in Dakar: flags flying, throngs of black people cheering. The bearded MALCOLM is smiling and responding to the cheers.

A very young black STUDENT, male, with a bright and eager face, is speaking to him.)

STUDENT *You must return. You must come back to us.*

MALCOLM *I* have *come back. After many centuries.*

Thank you—thank you!—for welcoming me. You have given me a new name!

(MALCOLM, in a great hall, somewhere in Africa, being draped in an African robe.

The black ruler, who places this robe on him, pronounces this new name at the same time that MALCOLM repeats it to the STUDENT.)

MALCOLM *Omowale.*

STUDENT *It means: the son who has returned.*

MALCOLM *I have had so many names—*

(We see the Book of the Holy Register of True Muslims. A hand inscribes in this book the name: *El-Haji Malik El Shabazz.*

We see a family Bible and a black hand inscribing: *Malcolm Little, May 19, 1925.*)

I will come back to you. I promise—(After a moment) *God willing.*

(The windows of New York buildings, blinding where the sun strikes.)

MALCOLM'S VOICE OVER *So many names—*

(We hear the raucous sound of a Lindy Hop.

In the side-view mirror: a conked and sweating
MALCOLM, dancing, spinning.

A voice yells, "Hey, Red! Go on, Red!"

MALCOLM acknowledges this, without missing a
beat. He is dancing with a very young, radiant, black girl,
LAURA. They execute a particularly spectacular and pun-
ishing *pas de deux*, the crowd roaring them on, and
when MALCOLM has, literally, set LAURA's feet on solid
ground again, he holds her against him a moment. They
are very, very young: and they smile at each other that
way.)

MALCOLM   *You are the cutest thing.*

(MALCOLM's present, weary, bearded face: very
much alone. Idly, he watches a very attractive blond girl
striding along the avenue.)

MALCOLM'S VOICE OVER   *Sophia—*

(The car stops for a light.

The blond girl, who is actually not SOPHIA, enters a
jewelry shop. We see her through the glass.

In the side-view mirror, we see:

MALCOLM's long hands tangled in SOPHIA's long
blond hair. They kiss—a long moment—and then we see
that they are in a room, on a bed. SOPHIA is wearing a
loose robe. MALCOLM is naked to the waist.)

MALCOLM *And what you going to tell your white boy about your black boy? your fine black stud? your nigger?—You hear me talking to you, Miss Anne?*

SOPHIA *I am not going to speak about you at all.*

MALCOLM *Suppose somebody else tells him?*

SOPHIA *Who could make him believe it?*

MALCOLM (laughs) *You keep telling me you know how white men are.* (She kisses him.) *Don't nobody care about you people at all?*

(He pulls her down on top of him. She buries her head in his chest. Then she looks up at him.)

SOPHIA *I don't think so—don't laugh—only you—*

(And MALCOLM pulls her head down on his chest.)

(MALCOLM, in prison, in a fist-fight. He and his opponent are separated by the guards.
A voice yells, "*Satan!*")

MALCOLM (shouting) *I didn't do a damn thing! I was minding my own business when this joker come fucking over me! I ain't no punk!*

(The GUARDS subdue him and hurl him into solitary, MALCOLM shouting and cursing every inch of the way. When the door locks behind him, he begins beating on the door, finally slumps.)

MALCOLM'S VOICE OVER   *So many names.*

(A tree, from which flutter old, discolored rags—which once were clothes, which once were bloodstained; great birds circling in a luminous gray sky; and then clothes billowing from the clothesline of the Little home.

A lone female black voice, singing:
"Bye and bye,
Bye and bye,
I'm going to lay down
This heavy, heavy load."

The very fair, young mulatto woman, pregnant, trudges from the clothesline toward this house. This is LOUISE LITTLE.

The one-eyed EARL LITTLE, preaching.)

EARL   *God has sent us a prophet who will take us home. Do you understand that, brothers and sisters? do you understand that? To take us* home! *Back to Africa! We're going to leave this accursed people, who been slaughtering us so long!* (His listeners all are black: a not overwhelming number. We are in a black church.) *But we must raise ourselves so that we need nothing from the white man—nothing!*

(Holster of a white man on horseback. The horse is restless.

From within a white house a black hand lifts a white curtain, lets the curtain drop.)

A BLACK VOICE *Lord have mercy.*

EARL *We shall establish our own businesses, raise our own food—*

(LOUISE, at the stove, cooking: and watching the clock.)

EARL *And when we have established our sufficiency, we will do as Christ told us to do—we will shake the dust of this most accursed of nations from off our feet. And join our brother, Marcus Garvey, and go home!*

(The Klan, riding through the night.

LOUISE hears this. She looks quickly at the children, who are silent.

The clothes on the line, billowing over the heads of some of the riders as they enter the Little yard.

LOUISE walks to the door, and faces the riders. LOUISE is nearly as white as they are and this lends her a very particular bitterness and a contemptuous authority. . .

If they are intimidated by the particular quality of her fury, they are nevertheless together and she is alone.)

LOUISE *What you all want here, this time of night? I got my children's supper on the stove.*

A RIDER *Where's your husband?*

LOUISE *If he was home, would I be standing out here in the yard?*

A RIDER *If you want to keep on standing, you better watch your tongue.*

LOUISE *You can veil your face, but you can't hide your voice, Mr. Joel. I know every one of you.*

(A RIDER laughs. His horse rears.)

A RIDER *Well, if you know every one of us, you know we mean business. You tell your one-eyed liver-lipped preacher husband—*

LOUISE *You tell him whatever it is you got to tell him! or ain't you man enough?*

A RIDER *We trying to be patient—*

A RIDER *You half-white bitch—*

LOUISE   *I might be your daughter, for all you know—*
        or your sister—!

A RIDER   *Your husband keep on stirring up the bad nig-*
         gers in this town, we going to have his ass in a sling
         —you tell him that!

A RIDER   *He going to lose his other eye!*

(His restless horse rears again, and, in a sudden
fury, the RIDER smashes in one of the windows with the
butt of his gun. He prods his horse, and all the RIDERS
follow him. They ride around the house, smashing in
every window with their gun butts, and ride away.

LOUISE's clenched hands on her swollen belly.)

(Night. The streetcar tracks, from the motorman's
point of view.

EARL rushes to catch this streetcar but misses it. He
stands, in an odd and violent frustration, on the tracks,
watching the streetcar vanish. He begins walking home.

A car with Nebraska license plates moves slowly
along the dark streets, and we see that the two white
men in the car are armed.

EARL walks under the billowing clothesline, and
the light falls on his face as his wife opens the door. He
walks slowly around his violated house; we hear the
children whispering and weeping.

He turns to LOUISE, who stands in the doorway, who has not moved.)

LOUISE   *Earl, maybe now you'll listen to me. We can't stay here. Earl. We got to go.*

EARL   *I ain't going to let them drive me away like this. —Oh, no. Oh, no.*

LOUISE   *Listen to your children in there, crying, scared to death! Man, can't you hear your children?*

EARL   *I hear my children. That's why we ain't going to run.*

(He starts into the house. LOUISE stops him.)

LOUISE   *Earl, it don't matter about me. I ain't worried about me. I ain't never asked for you to worry about me. We made our choice, and that's all right. But my babies, Earl—my babies!*

(She is weeping. He holds her to him, a long moment; we watch his face.)

EARL   *All right. Tell you what. We'll go. We'll go. But we can't go nowhere tonight. I got to get busy fixing these windows. And tomorrow morning—early to-*

morrow morning—*I'll start arranging for us to get out of this town.—But it going to be the same thing, no matter where we go. They ain't never going to treat us right, not here. This white man is too sick. We got to get to Africa.*

LOUISE   *Earl—where in Africa?*

EARL   *Wherever Brother Garvey leads us.*

LOUISE   *I wish I was black—black like you—blacker than you! Goddamn it, how I hate them, hate them—! Every drop of that white rapist's blood that's in my veins!*

EARL   *Hush.* (He strokes her belly.) *We can't get far, nohow, before this little one gets here. He in a hurry. I can feel him pushing up against my hand.*

LOUISE   *He'll sure be here before we get to Africa.*

(They go into the house.
We see a map, and LOUISE's finger.)

LOUISE'S VOICE OVER   *No. You were born here, Malcolm.* (Her finger touches: Omaha.) *And then we moved—here.*

(Her finger touches: Milwaukee.)

(Night. The screen is dark. A match is struck in the darkness. It flickers, seems nearly to go out; then another wisp of flame appears; then another.

EARL turns in bed, beginning to awaken.

LOUISE sits up.)

LOUISE *Earl!*

(The flames are devouring the house. They gather up the children, covering them with blankets, with anything, and get them out of the house.)

EARL *We got all the children? Where's Malcolm?*

LOUISE *He's here. They're all here.*

A CHILD'S VOICE *Here I am.*

(We watch EARL's desperate face, watching the fire.

LOUISE is watching.

The arrival of the fire engines. The firemen are white.

The crowd gathering. The crowd is white.

The fire trucks come to a halt; and the firemen stand and watch the fire.

EARL turns and watches the crowd. He picks up the baby, MALCOLM, and holds him in his arms.

Father and son, the mother and the children watch the crowd watching the fire.

A map.)

LOUISE'S VOICE OVER   *And then your father built a house—here.* (Her finger stops at: Lansing.) *That's where we stayed.*

(A sea gull, turning and turning in the sky. A bright summer day.

The young, bright, gawky, conked MALCOLM, walking, with his shoes and a pair of girl's shoes tied over his shoulder.)

MALCOLM   *I wasn't really born there. I just grew up there.*

LAURA   *I never heard of it.*

MALCOLM   *Well, there's a big town not too far from it, called Detroit—that's where they make the cars. You ever hear of Detroit?*

(MALCOLM and LAURA are walking along a deserted Cape Cod beach, barefoot, he with his trousers rolled.)

LAURA   *Yes. I've heard of Detroit. Was—Lansing—a nice town? Did you like it there?*

MALCOLM   *I didn't want to live there. No more than I want to live in Boston.*

LAURA   *What's wrong with Boston? I live here.*

MALCOLM   *Well, I think I'm big enough to overlook that. In fact, I'm thinking of kidnapping you. You want to be like all them hill clowns? them people your grandmother like so much?*

LAURA   *Just because my grandmother likes them doesn't mean that I have to like them.*

MALCOLM   *She want you to like them. She want you to be like that. She want you to marry somebody like that. Like that deacon—what's his name—so black and puffed up he can't hardly talk—the one who call me* Master Little*—ha! I ain't master of nothing. He say he "in banking." In banking!* (An elderly black man, solemnly winding an impressive watch.) *He don't see penny one in that bank. They don't let him nowhere near the money. All he do is mop their floors.* (Which, after the gentleman has elaborately tucked his watch away, we see is all too true.) *And old Miss Stella, talking about she with a "old family"—yeah. And what she doing with that old family? She cook their food and scrub their toilets—* (A handsome black woman is simultaneously putting on her street clothes and expertly filling a large,

14

respectable-looking handbag.)—*and take home their leftovers. If she married to that cat "in banking," I reckon she better.*

LAURA *Don't talk like that.*

MALCOLM *Well, it's true! And that cat "in utilities." He in, all right—when he ain't outside riding a bicycle for the gas company. In utilities!*

LAURA *That's another generation. You haven't got to be like that.*

MALCOLM (stops walking; looks at her) *You' damn right.*

LAURA *Oh—!* (Suddenly, she grabs his hand and starts running with him. They start laughing. They run to the water's edge and fall down, laughing, in the sand.) *Oh, look!*

MALCOLM *Look at what?*

(But he follows her finger and sees what she sees: the sea gull, turning and swooping in the sky.)

LAURA *He wears the sky like an overcoat.*

MALCOLM (looks at her, amused and moved) *Honey,*

he's just looking for food. He got a lot of mouths to feed.

LAURA   *You're always so—practical.*

MALCOLM   *I better be.*

(He kisses her, lightly, playfully, like a brother, and sits up. He takes their shoes off his shoulders and rests them on the sand.)

LAURA   *It's peaceful here.*

MALCOLM   *You think so? I wish it was. I wish I could make it peaceful for you. I guess I'd do anything for you—if I could do anything—*

LAURA   *But you can, Malcolm, you can! You—you could be a wonderful man.*

MALCOLM   *You know, when I was a little boy, where we lived*—(He pauses, to be reassured by LAURA, who is lying on her side, watching him.) *I ain't never really told you about where we lived, but it was in the country—and we grew our own food— that was my daddy's idea—*(We watch LAURA, watching MALCOLM.)—*and so we had our own garden, you know, and so I asked my mama if I could have my own little garden, too. And so she said, Yes, and she let me. I loved it and I took care of it. I used to love to grow peas. I used to be proud when we had them on the table—on our table—*

(LOUISE, smiling, humming, shelling peas.)

MALCOLM'S VOICE OVER *I used to crawl on my hands and knees, looking for the bugs and the worms and then I'd kill them and bury them.* (We see the ground very close, as if from the viewpoint of a crawling child, and remain fascinated before one enormous green shoot.) *And sometimes I would lie down on my back between my nice clean rows and gaze up at the blue sky at the clouds moving—*

(MALCOLM's face.)

MALCOLM *—and think all kind of things.*

LAURA *What kind of things?*

MALCOLM *All kinds of things. I used to dream that I would be speaking to great crowds of people—and I would somehow do something which would help my father and my mother. I didn't want my mother to work so hard.* (We watch LAURA watching MALCOLM. He suddenly grabs her hand and looks up at her.) *They used to fight because they both worked too hard.*

(The blue sky, from the viewpoint of someone lying on his back.)

LOUISE'S VOICE OVER   *We ain't never ate rabbit before in this house, Earl!*

(The sky: very still.)

EARL'S VOICE OVER   *Well, we going to be eating rabbit today!*

(The sky goes out of focus, goes black for a moment, tilts out of sight, and LOUISE comes into focus.)

LOUISE   *We only raised rabbits to sell to white folks.*

EARL   *Did you hear what I just told you?*

(A rabbit, EARL's hands on its neck, being whirled around and thrown to the floor.
   LOUISE is horrified, sweating, speechless.)

EARL   *Fix it for dinner. I be back soon.*

(LOUISE looks at the rabbit at her feet picks it up, puts it on the sink, finds a knife.
   EARL leaves the kitchen, and the yard.
   LOUISE walks from the darkness of the kitchen into the brightness of the yard.)

LOUISE *Earl!*

(EARL turns to face her: in focus, though already quite far away. LOUISE has her back to us.)

LOUISE *Earl—?*

(EARL waves his hand, and, after a moment, turns and walks away. We watch him—still from the point of view of LOUISE—vanish from our sight.

MALCOLM is still holding LAURA's hand.)

MALCOLM *Are you cold?*

LAURA *No.*

MALCOLM *You were shivering.*

LAURA *Every time you touch me, makes my blood run cold.*

(They laugh. He kisses her, lightly, playfully, as before. Then, suddenly, they really kiss, pull away, staring at each other with fear and wonder, and kiss again. MALCOLM pulls away.)

MALCOLM *You're the nicest girl I ever knew.*

LAURA *You're the nicest boy.*

MALCOLM   *Oh, I'm not nice. I'm not nice at all. Your grandma's right about me. You should listen to her.*

LAURA   *I have a mind of my own, Malcolm. I'm not a child.*

MALCOLM   *Yes, you are. Compared with me, you are. I don't come from around here. You don't know anything about me. Maybe everything I ever told you was a lie.*

LAURA   *I don't know anything about you? I know you're smart and distinguished—and—you're very nice.*

MALCOLM   *Will you come dance with me at the Roseland—Saturday night? I know your grandma gone have a fit.*

LAURA   *You name the night. I'll handle the fit.*

MALCOLM   (after a moment)   *It's time we was going.* (He kisses her on the cheek, very sorrowfully.) *Come on.*

(We watch them walk away, becoming very small figures, between the sea and the land, the sky.)

(MALCOLM's garden. Night.
We travel slowly through MALCOLM's rows.

The sky: dark.

LOUISE, at the stove, and watching the clock.)

EARL'S VOICE OVER (in the rythmn of the clock) *Sepa-rate! Separate! Leave this accursed land! Separate!*

A BLACK VOICE *Lord, have mercy.*

(The town: empty, dark.

Into this silence: the clanging of the streetcar bell.

The badly beaten body of EARL LITTLE lands heav-ily on the tracks. He tries to move; he cannot.

The clanging bell grows louder.

EARL's mouth opens in terror.)

(The frosted office door of an insurance company. LOUISE walks through this door.

LOUISE is facing a white man, who sits behind his desk.)

LOUISE *You know as well as me that my husband's pol-icy was paid up. He worked and suffered and starved to keep up on that policy!*

THE MAN *Mrs. Little, we do not deny that. But you must try to understand our problems, too. Our investiga-tors inform us that your husband met his death at his own hand. And, in that case, we cannot pay the policy. And that is the law. I deeply regret it—but my hands are tied.*

LOUISE   *The law!*

THE MAN   *But it is the law, Mrs. Little. You may—indeed you do—have all my sympathy. But I am not the law.*

LOUISE   *You can sit there and fix your mouth to tell me that my husband picked up a hammer and slammed it in the back of his own head and then dragged his body across the streetcar tracks? How a man going to beat in the back of his own skull?*

THE MAN   *Your husband's body was found lying across the streetcar tracks. Our verdict is suicide.*

LOUISE   *Suicide.*

(THE MAN *rises.*)

THE MAN   *I'm very sorry, Mrs. Little. I'm afraid there's nothing we can do.*

LOUISE   *You got any children?*

THE MAN   *I have—three little boys.*

LOUISE   *And you got life insurance. When one of them cuts your throat to get it, you just remember me.*

(Early in the morning, in the well-appointed kitchen of a white woman.)

WHITE WOMAN   *Why, I no more thought of you as his wife—excuse me, his widow—of that—I thought you were white—saying nothing is the same thing as lying—that rabble-rousing—I'm sorry, I'm a mother, too. But you'll have to go.*

LOUISE   *I hope I live long enough to hear somebody say them words to you. And maybe I will.*

(In the very different kitchen of the Little home, LOUISE is facing an earnest, young, white welfare worker, MISS DUNNE.)

MISS DUNNE   *Mrs. Little, you remember—sometime ago, when you lost your husband—*

LOUISE   *When my husband was murdered.*

MISS DUNNE   *You will remember that we discussed—*

LOUISE   *You. Not we.*

MISS DUNNE   *—the advisability, perhaps—*

LOUISE   *Of me sending my children away. And I said*
           then, and I say now, that you'd already robbed
           these children of their daddy and I wasn't going
           to let you rob them of their mother. Now, what you
           doing here, this morning?

MISS DUNNE   *We are only concerned with the welfare of*
               the children—we want to make sure that they are
               properly cared for—

LOUISE (laughs)   *If you could hear yourself—!*

MISS DUNNE   *Mrs. Little—*

LOUISE   Y*ou* *want to make sure—make sure—how did*
           you put it, you college-educated, dried-up, cat-
           faced, white bitch? —what did you say—you want
           to take care of my *children? I'd tear you limb from*
           limb before I'd give my children over to you, or
           anybody who looks like you. I can take care of my
           children.

MISS DUNNE   *We have reports on all of your children,*
               Mrs. Little, all of them are delinquent—and one of
               them is a thief—

LOUISE   *Is what?*

MISS DUNNE   *A—thief—Mrs. Little.*

LOUISE *Get out of my house.*

MISS DUNNE *Mrs. Little—*

LOUISE *Out, I say!*

MISS DUNNE *You'll regret this, Mrs. Little.*

LOUISE *If you don't move out this open door, you soon
going to be past all regretting.*

MISS DUNNE *I think you must be crazy.*

LOUISE *I got my kids to feed. I ain't going to let you
drive me crazy.*

(In the asylum: a ravaged LOUISE.)

LOUISE *Don't you let them feed that boy no pig.*

(The untidy back of the young, untidy MALCOLM's
head, sitting in a moving car, between two white OFFI-
CIALS.)

1ST OFFICIAL *Now, you just remember, boy, you lucky.
This ain't the reform school. This is just a nice private home. A real nice couple runs it, and you'll
go to school, and all, and nobody'll bother you just*

as long as you keep your nose clean—we giving
you a chance to make something of yourself, boy.

2ND OFFICIAL   *You're on probation, like they told you*
in the court. You know what that means? (He looks
over to MALCOLM, who does not answer.) *Look, kid.*
Your mother's just tired. It's only natural. She'll be
all right. (Silence.) *Okay. It's rough. But keep your*
nose clean.

(A dining room table, five surly white youths,
seated. They come closer and closer, staring up at MAL-
COLM—at us.)

MRS. SWERLIN'S VOICE OVER   *This is Malcolm—Mal-*
colm—Malcolm Little! our new guest. He's just
like all the rest of us and we're going to treat him
just like a brother, now, you hear?

(But the boys, as we can gather from their reaction
to this cheerful species of blackmail, are totally unable to
do this on command.)

(A furiously grieving, silent MALCOLM, chopping
wood.

MALCOLM, washing dishes.

MALCOLM, weaving, dribbling, dancing across the
basketball court, rising high in the air, seeming to fly,
as he makes the basket, which wins the game.

26

A sweating, grinning, exhilarated MALCOLM, in the locker room, surrounded by the ecstatic basketball team, of which he is the only black member. They are very proud of him, and very affectionate. Just as this sequence ends:)

VOICE OVER   *Where's Malcolm?*

(We are at the school dance, panning through the white boys and girls, dancing or flirting in the darkness outside. MRS. SWERLIN sits on the sidelines.)

PAUL (a young white student: laughs)   *He can't dance.*

(Night. The Negro section of Lansing. A black bar, loud music, laughter, men and women.
A very dressed-up MALCOLM, wandering the streets and entering this bar. He walks to the jukebox, drops in a coin, stands there until his record begins to play.
MALCOLM's face, tentative, eager, smiling, in shadows.)

A WOMAN'S VOICE OVER   *Honey, I know you ain't twenty-two, like you claim. But you sure is big for your age.*

(MALCOLM, raking leaves. He does this quietly, stolidly, thoroughly. He puts them in a pile; he sets

27

them aflame. Then he stands very still, looking not at the flames but at the sky.

From within the house, we watch MRS. SWERLIN watching him.)

MRS. SWERLIN (calls) *Malcolm.*

(MALCOLM, in the kitchen, peeling potatoes. MRS. SWERLIN is at the oven, baking, checking the progress of whatever is in the oven; then at the sink, etc.; near the end of this scene, she sits down, facing MALCOLM.)

MRS. SWERLIN *Oh, you would have liked my father, Malcolm. He came here from the old country and I guess he must have had clothes on his back because they let him in—but that's about all he had. But he was a stubborn man, and hard as a flint-stone. Of course, he wasn't hard with us. We knew how to get around him. I think girl children get on better with their daddy than boy children, don't you, Malcolm?*

MALCOLM *I don't know, Mrs. Swerlin.*

MRS. SWERLIN *But you got on all right with your daddy, didn't you?*

MALCOLM *Oh. Sure. I guess so.*

MRS. SWERLIN *You guess so?*

MALCOLM   *I mean—yes, ma'am. We got on fine.*

MRS. SWERLIN   *I guess you—people say all kinds of things about your daddy. But I don't listen. My father taught me better than that. The way my father was, well, if he was your friend, he was your friend. That's all there was to it. He didn't listen to what people said. Don't you think that's the way to be?*

MALCOLM   *Yes, ma'am.*

MRS. SWERLIN   *If there was more people like that, this world would be a better place, I bet you. How you getting along with the other boys?*

MALCOLM   *Oh, we get along fine.*

MRS. SWERLIN   *They're nice boys. Oh, they get out of hand every once in a while, wouldn't be human if they didn't—but they right nice lads. I ain't never been able to have none of my own, you know. It wasn't the Saviour's will. So I got me a houseful of other people's children, because everybody gets in trouble. People forget our Saviour was in trouble. You got any news from your mother?*

MALCOLM   *No, ma'am.*

MRS. SWERLIN   *You write to her?*

MALCOLM   *No, ma'am—I don't think they let her have no mail.*

MRS. SWERLIN   *Malcolm—a boy has one mother. I know that. And no one can take her place. And I wouldn't try. But I feel like a mother to you. And we're all very proud of you here. Yes, sir. You can bet your life on that. I ain't seen many boys, white or black, like you. You've got a lot on the ball, Malcolm, and I just know you can make something of yourself and you'll always have firends. You know why?*

MALCOLM   *No, ma'am.* (She lifts his chin. For a moment, they watch each other.) *Why?*

MRS. SWERLIN   *Because you're a friend. You treat people kind. People like to be around you. Everybody's noticed that. You must remember—you keep that spirit and you can be anything you want to be.— Tell you what. I know you kind of lonesome here, sometimes. It's only natural for you to want to see your people. Tell you: Fridays and Saturdays, after your work's finished, go on and take the bus to Lansing, see your friends. I know you won't get into no trouble, now, will you, Malcolm?*

MALCOLM   *No, ma'am.—Thank you, Mrs. Swerlin.*

(Night. The Negro section of Lansing. The bar.
MALCOLM and SHORTY, sitting in a booth.

SHORTY is—short; much darker than MALCOLM;
and a little older.)

SHORTY   No. I just didn't think I could take it no more,
cousin.

MALCOLM   So what are you going to do now?

SHORTY   Hustle me up another slave, I reckon—this
town, man!

MALCOLM   It ain't so bad—is it?

SHORTY   Oh, shit, I forgot, you been over there with all
them ofays so long you wouldn't even know.

MALCOLM   I ain't thinking about them ofays.—You
know what I'm thinking about.

SHORTY   Homeboy, you are a clown. A natural clown.
These broken-down black bitches around here, they
glad to give you some pussy, have you working
out like a champion, man, hollering about oh, it's
good, it's good, Daddy, time you ready to drop they
just belch and want some more. You clown. You
know why? Because you young and you dumb and
they really think you white.

31

MALCOLM   *Shorty, you sound like you jealous—or
         something.*

SHORTY   *I ain't jealous.*

MALCOLM   *Why you jumping salty on me, then?*

SHORTY   *The bitch puts out for you for free. Where
         she do it? In the room I pay for. She bring you your
         eggs in bed. Where she get the eggs? Huh? She say,
         Baby, have another drink. Where she get the bottle?
         Then she powder and perfume you and she send
         you home just before I get home with, maybe, even
         a little change in your pockets—*

MALCOLM   *Shorty, I ain't never had nothing to do with
         none of your women! What you telling me?*

SHORTY   *Nothing. But all that shit she give away, it
         comes off my black ass. I got to stand for somebody
         to call me nigger, every day, all day, so I can
         bring home the shit she give away to you for free,
         because she really thinks you white.*

MALCOLM   *Well, she might think I'm white—*

SHORTY   *Oh, you kind of think so, too. I can't really
         blame you. They got you kind of turned around,
         over at that school—and, over here, these black*

bitches think you cute—(MALCOLM, involuntarily, grins.) *Yeah. You wait till you start slaving out here, baby.*

MALCOLM   *They might make me Class President. I got the best grades, honest, and I'm very popular.*

SHORTY   *You are?*

MALCOLM   *Yeah. Everybody says so.*

SHORTY   *Yeah?*

MALCOLM   *Well, look, it ain't just a matter of being black. Nobody can help being black. But—everybody can be somebody—!*

SHORTY   *Yeah.*

MALCOLM   *Shorty you think I'm wrong?*

SHORTY   *I think I'll move on up to Boston. I ain't going to be able to get no more jobs in this town.*

MALCOLM   *What you going to do in Boston?*

SHORTY   *Be somebody.*

(Evening. The study of the SWERLIN home.

33

MALCOLM enters the SWERLIN study, to face MRS.
SWERLIN, and a stranger, JUDGE MERRITT.

MRS. SWERLIN is radiant.)

MRS. SWERLIN *Oh, we've got such good news for you,*
Malcolm—you tell him, Judge. Malcolm, you re-
member Judge Merritt?

MALCOLM *Yes, ma'am. How do you do, sir?*

(MALCOLM smiles, and the JUDGE nods.)

JUDGE MERRITT *Well, son, you know that you've been*
staying with the Swerlins kind of on probation, you
might say. After it was judged necessary to send
your mother away—because she was unable prop-
erly to take care of her children—(MALCOLM is
rigid, excessively attentive.)*—well you presented*
something of a problem, too. Looked like you were
about to take the wrong path there, for a while. You
remember we were thinking of sending you to re-
form school—you remember, boy?

MALCOLM *Yes, sir. I remember.*

MRS. SWERLIN *The Board had a meeting this afternoon,*
Malcolm—

JUDGE MERRITT   *The Board had a meeting and it was
    decided, in view of the amazing progress you have
    made with the Swerlins—your fine scholastic record
    and the phenomenal improvement in your, ah, char-
    acter—that it will not be necessary to send you to
    reform school. It is the judgment of the Board that
    you have reformed yourself.*

MRS. SWERLIN   *Didn't I tell you, Malcolm? Didn't I
    tell you? Oh, I'm so proud of you—so proud—just
    like you were my own—!*

MALCOLM   *Thank you. Thank you, sir. Thank you, Mrs.
    Swerlin.*

MRS. SWERLIN   *I didn't do it, Malcolm. You did it. Oh!
    your mother would be so proud of you!*

JUDGE MERRITT   *We're all proud of you. You keep it
    up, you hear?*

MALCOLM   *I surely will, sir. Thank you. Thank you.*

(They turn away from him. The moment their backs
are to him, MALCOLM, irrepressibly, executes a jubilant
dance.

    JUDGE MERRITT and MRS. SWERLIN are walking
toward the living room.)

JUDGE MERRITT   *I was walking through the nigger sec-tion of town today. I declare, I don't know how those people live—sometimes I wonder if they are peo-ple—*

MRS. SWERLIN   *Sometimes I wonder, too—of course, I know that God made everybody—*

JUDGE MERRITT   *—the children are filthy, the shacks just falling down around their heads—they can't fix the shacks but they got the big, shiny cars out front—*

MRS. SWERLIN   *I just don't know how niggers can be so happy and be so poor.*

(We watch MALCOLM's reaction to this, as the living room doors shut off MRS. SWERLIN and JUDGE MERRITT.
MALCOLM walks to a mirror, and stares at himself.
In the side-view mirror:
MALCOLM's fingers in SOPHIA's long blond hair.
MALCOLM, cursing and pounding on the cell door, in solitary.)

(Night. School buildings loom in the background. The building in which the dance is taking place is very brightly lighted; we hear the music and the voices.
MALCOLM is standing beneath a tree, with the white

36

student, PAUL. MALCOLM is watching him with curiosity and contempt.)

PAUL   —*no kidding, she told me that. Well, hell, all the girls around here are crazy about you, Malcolm. You make them hot, man, no kidding.* (MALCOLM says nothing. He looks a little frightened.) *Now, when I bring her out, man, you just sort of come along with us, okay? and you get in the car with us and I'll stop somewhere and make out like I have to pee—and I will, too—and I'll leave you and her in the car—and you can make your own arrangements—ha-ha and no harm done—and she'll get what she wants. She don't want it from me, man.* (Punches MALCOLM on the shoulder. MALCOLM flinches.) *She wants it from you.*

MALCOLM   *What do you want? You want to watch? Or you want it from me, too?*

PAUL   *Hey, what's the matter, man? All I'm doing is letting you know about some fine pussy—just waiting for you—*

MALCOLM   *How you know it's fine pussy? You say you ain't never had it. You just want me to get it ready for you—because you know if she puts out for me, she going to* have *to put out for you—*(MALCOLM

37

laughs.) *I got you dead to rights that time, didn't I, man?* (Stops laughing.) *You punk.*

(Day. MR. OSTROVSKI's office.

MR. OSTROVSKI is a young teacher, with a fairly intelligent, sensitive face. He is working alone in his office, and he looks up as we—that is, MALCOLM—approach.)

MR. OSTROVSKI *Come in, Malcolm, come in, my boy. I'm always glad to see you. I probably shouldn't tell you, but you're one of my favorite students—hell, you know that, anyway. What's on your mind?*

MALCOLM *I overheard some of the other students, sir, asking your advice about their futures—after we graduate from here, sir. And I wanted to get your advice about—about—about me—about my future.*

(But, for some reason, watching MR. OSTROVSKI, he begins to be afraid.)

MR. OSTROVSKI *Well, if I can advise the others, I suppose I can advise the Class President. I hope I can, anyway.*

MALCOLM *Well, sir, I've been looking around me and trying to figure out what I'm best suited to do—and —and—well, I really want to make something of*

*myself, sir, and I—well, everybody seems to feel
that I have a logical mind—and they seem to think
that I talk well and am kind of presentable—well—
the subject which really interests me is—law. You
must have noticed how much I like to argue—*(MAL-
COLM *tries to laugh, but* MR. OSTROVSKI *does not
laugh.*) *Well—I think I'd like to try to be a lawyer,
sir. And I wanted to ask your advice as to how to go
about it—the best schools, and so forth—*

(The silence stretches. MALCOLM sits very still. MR.
OSTROVSKI rises and paces.)

MR. OSTROVSKI   *I think it my duty to tell you something
very difficult, Malcolm. I hope you'll understand me
and take it in the spirit in which it's offered.* (MR.
OSTROVSKI *sits down, facing* MALCOLM.) *The most
important thing about anybody's life—the key, I
think, to any really successful life—is for the person whose life it is to be realistic about it. Hell,
when I was little, I wanted to be a fireman. But
I'm afraid of fire—you understand me? When I was
a young man, I wanted to be a movie star—but
my face would break the camera—*(Now, OSTROV-
SKI *laughs, but* MALCOLM *is silent.*) *What I'm trying
to say is that it's foolish to have ambitions which
can never be fulfilled. People who do that just end
up with a broken heart. And they become very dan-*

*gerous, to themselves and to others. Now, Malcolm,
do you know of any colored lawyers in this town—
do you?*

MALCOLM   *No.—Sir.*

MR. OSTROVSKI   *Colored people can't become lawyers,
Malcolm. That's all there is to it. And we've got
to be realistic. Believe me, I'm saying this for your
good. I don't want you to be hurt—that's the important thing—the important thing about a life is to
be realistic, Malcolm. Colored people can't become
lawyers. You know that. So, you have to decide to
do something a colored person can do.* (OSTROVSKI
rises and paces.) *Why don't you become a carpenter? You're very good with your hands—everybody's noticed that—and the people around here
would be happy to give you all kinds of work.* (MAL-
COLM stares at him.) *Do you understand me, son?*
(MALCOLM says nothing.) *You'll thank me for this
advice, one day.*

MALCOLM   *Thank you, sir.—Good-day, sir.*

(Day. The Boston Commons.
MALCOLM and SHORTY, walking. It is winter.
They pause before a monument.)

SHORTY   *Who is this cat? What did he do?*

MALCOLM   *He said, One if by land, and two if by sea—*

SHORTY   *That's what he said?*

MALCOLM   *Sure. He said: The British are coming.*

SHORTY   *That why they put him up there? On a horse?*

MALCOLM   *He was riding a horse. All over the country-side, man. He was warning the people.*

SHORTY   *Warning them about what?*

MALCOLM   *That the British was coming.*

SHORTY   *Was coming for what?*

MALCOLM   *Well, the Americans used to belong to England, man. But then they had a revolution—because they wanted to be free. You understand that? Yeah. You understand that. And the English didn't dig no revolution, so that's why they was coming. Didn't you go to school?*

SHORTY   *Maybe I wasn't paying attention. Where was we?*

MALCOLM   *Where was who?*

SHORTY   Us.

MALCOLM   *Oh. We was here. We was here, Daddy-o. Believe they got a statue someplace around here of some black motherfucker bared his breast to the English guns, man, and died, for freedom.*

SHORTY   *His widow get a pension?*

MALCOLM   *Don't believe he had no widow He was a slave. Slaves didn't have widows.*

SHORTY   *He was a fool.*

MALCOLM   *No, Shorty: he was a slave. But he's here, someplace. We was here.* (Laughs.) *Man, I bet you that cat was riding through the night, screaming, The niggers is coming! The niggers is coming!*

SHORTY   *Well, you know, that always wakes up the people.*

MALCOLM   *Man, we shouldn't joke about the Fathers of Our Country. It gives me a real bad choked-up feeling—*

SHORTY   *I know. Like a pain in the ass.* (The campus is deserted. They stand before the Harvard Law

School Forum.) *This is where they turn out all them lawyers—to help keep you and me in jail.*

(MALCOLM stares at this building. His face is very bitter. Carved on the facade is a Latin maxim meaning "Equal justice under the law."

Bells begin ringing. They are dismissal bells, resounding now across the campus, as the students, all of them white, pour out of the building. They scarcely see MALCOLM and SHORTY—they descend on the boys like waves breaking, and pass them with the same indifference—but they leave in their wake a very human resentment and wonder.

MALCOLM watches these students, with hatred in his eyes.

The bells change to: the clanging trolley-car bell.

The side-view mirror: the trolley-car comes closer and closer to the one-eyed man lying on the tracks.

EARL LITTLE's mouth opens in terror.

MALCOLM's face.)

MALCOLM   *So. What about this job you got fixed up for me?*

SHORTY   *Grin.* (MALCOLM bares his teeth. SHORTY, like an animal trainer, peers into his mouth.) *Them teeth is worth more than a college education.*

(A Lindy-Hop sound, loud: a white band's sound.

Night. The men's room of the Roseland Ball Room.
Attendants: MALCOLM and SHORTY.)

SHORTY   *Watch them—*

(We watch the dancehall patrons, noisy, white, and
well dressed.

MALCOLM is impressed and apprehensive.)

SHORTY'S VOICE OVER   *And watch me. Just remember:*
They love a happy darky. Just smile at them, baby,
show them all *your teeth, and they come in their*
pants. They so *happy to know you love them.* (A
white CUSTOMER returns from the urinal. SHORTY
has a basin of warm water waiting, and a towel
dangles from his waist.) *Dumbest motherfuckers*
in the world. (As MALCOLM watches, SHORTY ceremoniously extends the towel, which forces the CUS-
TOMER to use the water in the basin. The CUSTOMER
then reaches for the towel, and, as he dries his
hands, SHORTY begins brushing him off. He hums
and whistles as he is doing this.) *They like music,*
too. Cheerful music, like you so happy you just
can't keep it in.

(The CUSTOMER fishes for change.

SHORTY gives him a dazzling and yet subtly worried smile.)

44

SHORTY *I think you better let me hit them shoes a lick.*

(The CUSTOMER hesitates.

MALCOLM, emptying one basin and filling another, watches.)

SHORTY (smiles) *It don't pay to be in too great a hurry.*

(SHORTY leads the CUSTOMER to the shoeshine stand and gracefully gives him an arm up.)

SHORTY'S VOICE OVER *Now, the only thing to worry about is maybe the motherfucker's as broke as you.*

(SHORTY begins shining the CUSTOMER's shoes, to a syncopated beat, and whistling.)

SHORTY *I'm going to make 'em shine, Daddy-o!*

SHORTY'S VOICE OVER *And, man, just remember how they do love rhythm!*

(As SHORTY shines the shoes, we concentrate on the shoe rag and the shoe, and this movement becomes more frenetic.)

MALCOLM'S VOICE OVER *Mister, now you walking in double-barreled mirrors!*

CUSTOMER   *You on the ball, boy. Where you from?*

MALCOLM   *I'm from Detroit. People call me Red.*

CUSTOMER   *Well, you're one red-haired son of a bitch.*
(CUSTOMER steps down, fishing for change.) *You been working here long?*

MALCOLM   *Long enough, Daddy-o. All you got to do is name it*—(The music ends. The CUSTOMER watches MALCOLM with amusement.)—*and Detroit Red will supply it. I mean*—(The CUSTOMER is watching him. MALCOLM is watching the CUSTOMER watching.)—*should you get a little thirsty*—(MALCOLM touches his breast pocket.)—*or find that you have run out of an* indispensable *object*—(With a gesture too precise to be lewd, he indicates that he has a rubber stashed in his watch pocket.)—*or any other little thing*—(Lights a cigarette, takes a long drag, puts it in the ashtray, giving the CUSTOMER a long, level look)—*just come to Detroit Red.*

CUSTOMER   *You all right, boy. Best I've seen.* (Gives MALCOLM a coin, starts out, turns; in another tone, husky, conspiratorial.) *Suppose I wanted to try and change my luck—you know what I mean?*

MALCOLM   *It's a great big world, Daddy-o. Ain't nothing to it.*

(The CUSTOMER smiles again, winks, and tosses MALCOLM another coin.)

CUSTOMER   *Be seeing you, Red.*

   (Exit.)

MALCOLM (dry)   *I'll be here.*

SHORTY'S VOICE OVER   *Wait a minute now. Let's see.*

   (We are in a men's store, and SHORTY is considering MALCOLM, who is turning around in his first zoot suit.)

SHORTY   *Okay.*

   (In a shoe store mirror, a rather resounding pair of shoes walk toward us, walk away, turn, stop.)

SHORTY'S VOICE OVER   *How they feel, Homeboy?*

MALCOLM'S VOICE OVER   *Well, all reet!*

   (MALCOLM, staring into a mirror. Very gingerly, he places on his head a wide-brimmed hat—and smiles, pleased as only the very young can be, at his reflection. His face changes, as he hears, sharply:)

SHORTY'S VOICE OVER   *Take that off. Goddammit. I forgot the most important thing.*

(Day. SHORTY walks into a grocery store and very carefully selects: two eggs and two potatoes.

We follow him from this store into a drugstore. Here he purchases one large jar of Vaseline, one large-tooth comb and one fine-tooth comb and one large bar of soap.

We follow him into a hardware store, where he purchases a rubber hose with a metal spray-head, and a can of Red Devil lye, and one rubber apron and one pair of rubber gloves.

This is all accomplished in silence, in pantomime, and SHORTY is as solemn as an African chief.)

(Day. A barber shop. Five or six blacks, of various ages: one is in the barber's chair, actually getting a haircut. One man, very young, is reading a newspaper.

The others constitute a kind of hallelujah chorus, or amen corner, to the monologue of the stout, good-natured, middle-aged barber.)

BARBER   —*and I hit the number. Lord, why did I have to go and do that? You know that woman wasn't never no more good to me after that?* (The MEN laugh.) *She thought she was married to Cary Grant. And we wasn't even* married. *I always had better sense than* that. *She wanted me to buy her a* yacht.

(The MEN laugh again.) *I like to slapped that*
bitch upside the head. I said, Bitch, you don't
hardly never go near no bath tub, now what you
want with a yacht? She say, So I can push you off
the side, you cheap black motherfucker.—When a
black woman call you a black motherfucker, you
have been called a black motherfucker.—No. She
weren't no more good to me after that.—And the
money didn't last too long, neither, another bitch got
close to me, you know what I mean. I didn't buy
her no yacht, though.—Hey, Shorty!

SHORTY *Where's Homeboy? Ain't he got here yet?*

BARBER *Red's in the head, man. He'll be right out.*

(SHORTY solemnly removes his jacket and his hat,
and rolls up his sleeves. He places his materials on a
table.

The MEN watch him.

The BARBER hands SHORTY a Mason jar. SHORTY
peels the potatoes and "thin-slices" them into this jar.)

THE BOY READING THE NEWSPAPER *Going to lay that*
first conk on your Homeboy, Shorty?

SHORTY *Man, you see what I'm doing.*

(Indeed we do. Over the potatoes, he pours a little

over half the can of lye, stirring slowly with a wooden spoon.

The MEN have seen all this before, but are fascinated nonetheless.

We see the results of the wedding of the lye and the potatoes.

SHORTY breaks in two eggs, stirring very fast.

We see his sweating, intense face.

SHORTY looks up as the bathroom door slams, and motions to the BARBER.)

SHORTY   *Get him ready.* (MALCOLM appears, and stands looking apprehensively at SHORTY's handiwork.) *Come here.* (MALCOLM obeys.) *Touch this jar.* (MALCOLM touches the jar, and jumps. SHORTY laughs.) *Told you. You make sure and tell me if there's any stinging when I get through. This stuff can burn a hole in your head.*

(MALCOLM looks as though he doesn't doubt this; he also appears rather to regret that things have progressed so far.

The BARBER places him in the chair and puts the white cloth around him. SHORTY approaches with the congolene, and all the MEN now gather round to witness this species of ritual—which, for the frightened MALCOLM, is much closer to being a kind of execution.

Ceremoniously, SHORTY puts on the rubber apron and the rubber gloves. He first combs up MALCOLM's bushy hair and then massages a great quantity of Vaseline into his hair; and then he covers MALCOLM's ears, neck, and forehead with Vaseline.)

SHORTY   *Hold tight, now. It's going to burn like hell.*

(SHORTY starts combing in the congolene.

MALCOLM nearly leaps out of the chair, but is held down by the BARBER.

MALCOLM finally manages to catch enough breath to scream.)

MALCOLM   *Stop it, stop it, stop it, goddammit, you black motherfucker, stop it!*

(MALCOLM begins to weep and finally manages to break out of the chair.

The BARBER and one of the MEN hold him.

An utterly unmoved SHORTY follows MALCOLM with the hose, grabs MALCOLM's head, lathers it, and begins spraying his head.

SHORTY does this several times as MALCOLM's sobs and screams subside.

MALCOLM is wet and shaking: and they have made rather a mess of the barber shop.

SHORTY leads the parboiled MALCOLM back to the chair.)

SHORTY   *How does it feel? Does it feel like it's all out?*

MALCOLM   *Man, don't ask me how it feels—it feels like*
I ain't got no skin on my head, that's how it feels.
How the fuck can I tell if it's all in or all out?

(SHORTY begins toweling MALCOLM's hair.
MALCOLM begins shouting and cursing again.
The side-view mirror.)

LOUISE   *How I hate them—hate them!—every drop of*
that white rapist's blood that's in my veins!

(MALCOLM screams.)

EARL'S VOICE OVER.   *Hush.*

(SHORTY massages Vaseline into MALCOLM's hair
and combs it. MALCOLM is covered with sweat. He grits
his teeth and closes his eyes.)

THE MEN   *Yeah—!*

(MALCOLM opens his eyes, and is staring into a mirror.

We see a sweating and triumphant SHORTY reflected
in the mirror behind him.

MALCOLM's hair is as wavy as that of any white
movie star.

We watch his reaction to this incredible—indeed,
very nearly divine—transformation.

Tears are still standing in his eyes.)

MALCOLM   Hey—! *Hey, thanks, Shorty. Thank you, man.*

SHORTY   *Now, it was worth it, wasn't it? and you cursing me like that—*

(The MEN laugh.
MALCOLM wonderingly strokes his hair.)

MALCOLM   *Oh, yeah. Hell, yeah. It was worth it, all right.—I didn't mean to curse you.*

THE BOY   *Next time, it won't hurt so bad, you kind of get used to it.*

BARBER   *Hell, it's just like anything else, Red. First time you pop a cherry, you might be a little scared —but pretty soon there ain't nothing to it, ain't that so, Red?*

(The MEN laugh.
MALCOLM stares into the mirror.)

(The sound of Lionel Hampton's band.
The Roseland, as before: but, now, the patrons are black.)

53

SHORTY'S VOICE OVER *On the night the white people dance, we can't dance. I mean: we can't dance with them. But they can dance with us.*

(A black boy and girl are dancing, dominating the floor, to the great enthusiasm of the spectators.

A very expensively dressed, very attractive blond girl—SOPHIA—moves to the front line of the spectators in order to get a better view of the dancers.

MALCOLM and LAURA are also on the sidelines.)

MALCOLM *Your grandma didn't have a heart attack? or fall down on her knees and start praying? or call the police?*

LAURA *You stop making fun of my grandma. At least she appreciated that I was telling her the truth.*

MALCOLM *And how'd you put it to her?*

LAURA *I just said that I was coming out with you, to the Roseland, and I thought she'd better hear it from me, tonight, than hear it from her friends tomorrow.*

MALCOLM *And then you blew on your trusty six-shooter and saddled Hyo Silver and came riding down to the valley.*

LAURA   *Shut up.*

MALCOLM   *I'm mighty glad you did.*

LAURA   *I am, too. I couldn't have done it if it hadn't been for you.*

MALCOLM   *Come on, girl. Let's show them how.*

LAURA   *Oh, Malcolm. I don't know if I can dance like that.*

MALCOLM   *You better get out of them shoes, girl. You got to wear them in church tomorrow.*

(LAURA laughs, and goes to a bench and changes into a pair of sneakers.

MALCOLM takes her onto the floor, and because of the competition, they begin at a very high speed.

The audience very quickly becomes aware of them and begins goading them on.

The other dancers move to the side of the floor, marking time, yielding the dance floor to MALCOLM and LAURA: who go into a solo.

We are aware that SOPHIA has singled out MALCOLM.

MALCOLM is only tangentially aware of SOPHIA, but is responding joyously to the response of the audience.

Finally, MALCOLM capers off the dance floor, LAURA

hanging limp around his neck, as the audience applauds.)

MALCOLM *Hey, you just about ready for the Cotton Club, ain't you? How you feel now?*

LAURA *Wonderful!—I'll be right back.*

MALCOLM *You are the cutest thing.*

(LAURA laughs, and goes.

The music begins again, and SOPHIA approaches MALCOLM, stretching out her arms to indicate that she wants to dance—for openers, anyway.

MALCOLM is very taken aback.

Wordlessly—rather like one hypnotized—he glides into SOPHIA's arms.

And immediately recognizes, through the eyes of the other men, that he has become the troubling center of attention. He has new status, because of SOPHIA. It gives him a heady feeling, because if this white girl is a whore, she is certainly a high-class one—only her hairdresser knows for sure!

LAURA returns. She can scarcely believe her eyes: is terribly frightened and hurt.)

SOPHIA *You're one hell of a dancer.*

MALCOLM *Thanks. You're not bad yourself.*

SOPHIA   *Would you rather be dancing with your girl—
the girl you brought?*

MALCOLM   *It's all right..She don't mind.*

SOPHIA   *She's a fool if she doesn't.—What's your name?*

MALCOLM   *People call me Red.*

SOPHIA   *Well, Red, why don't you take your little girl
home—she looks too young—and much too respec-
table—to be out with you, anyway—and come back
here, for me?*

MALCOLM   *Come back here for you?*

SOPHIA   *Yes. Come back here—for me.*

MALCOLM   *And what we fixing to do—when I come
back here for you?*

SOPHIA   *You seem to like music.—And I've got a radio
in my car.*

MALCOLM   *What's your name?*

SOPHIA   *People call me Sophia.*

MALCOLM   (softly, after a moment)   *Well—all reet
then!*

(Night. We are on the porch of LAURA's house.)

MALCOLM'S VOICE OVER   *I'd better not come in.*
(LAURA's face.)

MALCOLM   *I mean—it's late, baby. And I don't want
your grandmother raising cain.*

LAURA   *It's good of you to be so worried about my
grandmother.* (MALCOLM starts to kiss her, stops.
LAURA turns away.) *I know where you're going.*

MALCOLM   *I'm going to bed. I got to work tomorrow.*
(We see MALCOLM's head next to SOPHIA's, on the
dance floor: MALCOLM is very excited.) *Baby, I'll
call you, okay?*

(LAURA walks to her door.)

LAURA   *Sure. As soon as you find the time.* (LAURA is
very distressed, but is fighting it. A window opens
upstairs.) *It's just me, grandma. And it's—early.*

MALCOLM   *Goodnight, Mrs. Johnson. Goodnight, Laura.*

LAURA   *Goodnight.*

(MALCOLM runs down the porch steps.)

(Night. SOPHIA's wrap, on the floor of her car, il-
luminated by the light of the radio, which is playing a
tune like "Star Dust."

MALCOLM and SOPHIA, locked together, seeming to
wish to devour each other.

We remain with the radio until the light fades to
grey, and this radio becomes the radio on SOPHIA's night
table, next to her bed.

The radio announcer tells us that Pearl Harbor has
just been bombed by the Japanese.

In his demi-sleep, MALCOLM turns and clicks the
radio off, and moves closer to SOPHIA.

As MALCOLM turns in his sleep, we hear Lionel
Hampton's "Flying Home," and the sound of a speeding train.

We hear the beat of the shoe-shine rag: and we see
acres and acres of shoes being polished.

MALCOLM's face begins to be reflected in these moving shoes.

Over this: miles and miles of speeding, snarling,
railroad track.

The train windows: the American landscape kalei-
doscoping by.

The train interior: the American people, two-thirds
of them in uniform.)

MALCOLM'S VOICE OVER *Get your good ham and cheese*
    sandwiches! Ham and cheese! Chicken salad! Cof-
    fee! Tea! Coca-Cola! (MALCOLM's face, serving

and smiling. MALCOLM is in close-up throughout the following sequence.) *And I hope it kills you.*

VOICE OVER *Boy! Two ham and cheese!*

MALCOLM *Yes, sir. A little mustard, sir?*

MALCOLM'S VOICE OVER *Because you look like a real shit-eater to me.*

VOICE OVER *Boy! Can I have a Coke?*

MALCOLM *Yes, sir. Would you like a glass or a straw, sir?*

MALCOLM'S VOICE OVER *Or do you just want to tear it open with your teeth?*

VOICE OVER *Boy! This coffee's cold!*

MALCOLM *I'm terribly sorry, ma'am. I'll fix that right away, ma'am.*

MALCOLM'S VOICE OVER *I'll piss in it this time.*

(From the point of view of the motorman, the train surfaces out of the tunnel at Park Avenue and 99th Street.

The train stops at 125th Street, and MALCOLM, now

dressed in street clothes, slowly descends into the streets of Harlem.)

(Late afternoon. Small's Paradise.

It is a winter afternoon—a winter sun; and Small's is very quiet, with the quietness emanating from people who know exactly why they are where they are.

The people are much older than MALCOLM, a few women, but mostly men, quietly and expensively dressed, a few at the bar but mostly at the tables.

MALCOLM's arrival in his zoot suit causes something of a sensation among the people at the bar, who see him first.

WEST INDIAN ARCHIE and a few of his friends are sitting at a table quietly talking and drinking.)

MALCOLM   *A bourbon and water, sir.*

(The BARTENDER hesitates—MALCOLM does not realize that he is thinking of asking him for his draft card —and then decides.)

BARTENDER   *What kind of bourbon would you like, sir?*

MALCOLM   *What, sir?*

BARTENDER   *What brand of bourbon?*

(The bar is amused.)

MALCOLM *Oh! I'm sure you know more about it than I do, sir.*

(The bar silently cracks up.

The BARTENDER can think of no reply to this—dimly wonders, in fact, if MALCOLM isn't putting him on—and serves him.

MALCOLM sips his drink and looks about him with a wonder so honest that, while it is funny, it is also moving.

Now, he discovers the jukebox and moves toward it: which means that he passes WEST INDIAN ARCHIE's table: and these seasoned hustlers see him.

WEST INDIAN ARCHIE looks once, rubs his eyes, looks again. The table roars with laughter.

MALCOLM is oblivious. He has dropped in his coin and is digging Dinah Washington.

As the table watches him, their faces subtly change. All of them, in one way or another, have been MALCOLM once.)

ARCHIE *That boy thinks he's in heaven.*

CADILLAC *He sure is flapping them wings—and things.*

SAM *Remind me of you, when you come to the city.*

CADILLAC *You know damn well where you was, when I come to the city.*

ARCHIE *We all been there, Cadillac, ain't like it was something hard to do.* (MALCOLM leaves the juke-box, and, passing the table, narrowly misses stumbling over ARCHIE's feet.) *Them's forty-dollar Florsheims, boy.*

MALCOLM *Sir, I'm very sorry. I'm sorry.*

ARCHIE (after a moment) *It's all right. I got them at a discount.*

(The table laughs. MALCOLM goes back to the bar.)

CADILLAC *He ain't been there, yet.*

ARCHIE *No. He ain't been there. Yet.* (Goes to the bar. To the BARTENDER:) *Give Country-boy, there, a drink on me.*

BARTENDER *Reet.*

(ARCHIE returns to the table.)

CADILLAC *Now, what you got in mind, Archie?*

ARCHIE *Got a son somewhere, just about his age. Ain't never seen him, but it figures.*

SAM *Archie, if you going to start buying strangers drinks on that basis—*

CADILLAC *Leave him alone. He got more daughters than he got sons.*

(The BARTENDER serves MALCOLM.)

MALCOLM *But I didn't order another drink.*

BARTENDER *It's on the gentleman over there.—The one you kicked.*

MALCOLM *The one I—?*

(The split-second before he understands:)

ARCHIE (yells) *It's on me, Country-boy! Come on over here!*

MALCOLM *Yes, sir. Thank you, sir.* (Goes to the table.) *How did you know I was from the country?*

(Night. ARCHIE and MALCOLM, on the Harlem streets.)

ARCHIE *It seems to me that you don't feel exactly en-thusiastic about being a railroad man.*

MALCOLM *Well, sir, I don't think I can spend the rest of my life serving them people sandwiches. I don't*

*think I was cut out for that. But I don't know what
I was cut out for, neither.*

ARCHIE   *Well—a boy like you—he's kind of cut out for
—well, for whatever he can find. Whatever he can
make work for him. Because, you know, you got—
this—*(This is a habit of ARCHIE's: he touches the
back of his hand, to indicate the color of his skin.)
*And, when you got—this—ain't nothing made easy
for you. I reckon you've found that out, though.*

MALCOLM   *Yeah. Yes, sir. I have.*

ARCHIE   *Well, then, you got to grow up real quick;
don't, you won't grow up at all. You know what I
mean?*

MALCOLM   *Yes, sir. But I don't know how to start!*

ARCHIE   *Well, maybe I can give you a few pointers. I
been out here for a while.*

(We see the Harlem streets from ARCHIE's point of
view: and these streets change as he speaks.)

ARCHIE'S VOICE OVER   *I wasn't but a little crumb-
snatcher when we come here from the islands.
That's how I can dig what your father was thinking.*

(The Harlem of about 1912. The Harlem of that time was almost entirely white. The buildings, which have since become so dilapidated and despised, were, then, proud, private homes.) *We come here, looking for milk and honey—looking to live. But so many of us come—*

(A sign, reading "No Colored Need Apply," fades into a sign, reading "Colored Occupancy." A sign, reading "For Rent," fades into a sign reading "For Sale.")

—that the white folks packed up their milk and honey and run to another heaven—leaving this one to us. Or so it seemed. But heaven is always owned by white folks.

(The Cotton Club of the twenties: black entertainers, white audience.

Clip of Louis Armstrong and his horn.

Fats Waller and his piano.

A poetry reading: a few lines from Langston Hughes' "Life for Me Ain't Been No Crystal Stair."

Ethel Waters.

Bill Robinson.

The Tree of Hope, in the middle of Seventh Avenue.

A jam session at Minton's.

Pig-Feet Mary's.)

We kind of had it to ourselves for a while. We thought we did. But, if you don't own your heaven —it ain't heaven long.

(The playbill of the Lafayette Theater, fading into nothingness.

The boarded-up front of this theater.)

The profits from hell is also for white folks. But people got to live.

(Various Harlem citizens:

A weary matron, climbing the stairs, with a heavy shopping bag.

A janitor, setting out the garbage cans.

Adolescents, fighting on the street corner.

A lone whore, walking her beat.

A child, her hair being braided.

Superimposed, slowly, on these faces: an American dollar bill.

Filling the screen: In God We Trust.

Superimposed on this: the serial number of the bill.

The Stock Exchange Board, at the end of the day.

The last three figures on the Board.

A black church, the PREACHER in the pulpit.)

PREACHER *Dearly beloved, we take our text tonight from the Book of Job, Chapter 18, verses 17 and 18: His remembrance shall perish from the Earth—*

67

WOMAN'S VOICE OVER *That's one-eight-one and seven-one-eight.*

(A hand, writing combinations of these numbers on a scrap of paper.

A cash register, ringing up: $3.27.)

VOICE OVER *Three-two-seven.*

(A hand, writing this number on a scrap of paper.)

VOICE OVER *Yeah. What time your plane leave for Florida? Three forty-five? Yeah. Hey, what's the number on that flight—What?—no. Your flight number. Damn, girl, I know your height.—What— 103? Well, all root, have fun, bye!—345—103— Let's see—*

WOMAN'S VOICE OVER *Hattie, last night I was dreaming about the oyster boats we used to work on down home—what number do the dream book give for oysters?*

A GIRL'S VOICE OVER *Oh, I didn't hit for much, honey. But I got us a nice ham and some yams and a bottle of gin—because I know how much you love ham.— It taste all right, sugar?*

(During all of the foregoing, the screen is gradually filled with hands writing numbers on scraps of paper.)

(Night. MALCOLM and ARCHIE, in the back room of an after-hours joint. This joint is located in a private basement apartment.

The back room is divided from the drinking section by a locked door, which comes in and out of focus during the following scene: we hear, faintly, music and voices.

This room is dominated by a closet full of stolen goods, and ARCHIE is casually outfitting MALCOLM.)

ARCHIE   *And I never wrote down a number in my life. I keep it all in my head.—Get out of them pants, ain't nobody going take you seriously if you walk around looking like that. You see the way I dress, don't you? Try these, look like your size.—You see, Red, if you ain't got nothing on you, they can't take you in.—They look all right. Turn around.*

MALCOLM   *You mean—you keep all the combinations, everything, in your head, and you always remember who give you what number?—These look all right, sir?*

ARCHIE   *Ain't never made a mistake yet.—They feel all right in the waist?*

MALCOLM   *Yes, sir.—You must be some kind of mathematical genius. You ought to advertise.*

ARCHIE   *When a black man find a way of keeping alive,
he better not do no advertising.—I believe that's all
right. Try the jacket.*

MALCOLM   *It feels just right, sir. How do it look?*

ARCHIE   *Okay. Let's look over the shirts.—Another
thing. Don't never fuck with the poor. The poor is
dangerous. They ain't got nothing; they can't lose
nothing. Don't care how low things might get for
you, personally—these look like your size, try one
—when a number hits, you pay it. You pay every
number that hits. That way, the poor will protect
you.—That's good. Now, where he hiding his ties
and socks? Might be over here, I reckon.—Because, baby, you going to find out—you ain't got no
other protection out here.—I was right. Here they
are.—That man is on every black ass, baby, colder
than white on rice.*

MALCOLM   *You sure got it figured.*

ARCHIE   *The first time I was ever called a nigger, I
made haste to get it figured.—He out of hats. We'll
get you that tomorrow.—I think you almost ready
now. How you feel?*

MALCOLM   *Ready, sir.*

ARCHIE *Believe I'll buy you a drink. Come on.*

(And ARCHIE unlocks the door.)

(Night. MALCOLM, walking up Seventh Avenue, in the driving rain. He is walking very quickly, and turns into a corner bar. This is a very ordinary bar, quite unlike Small's, fairly crowded, both sexes, the young and the not so young.)

BARTENDER *Hey, Red. How you doing, baby?*

MALCOLM *Feel like I just drowned. How you doing?*

BARTENDER *Oh, I got a good holt on it. What you want?*

MALCOLM *Double bourbon, straight, no chaser.*

BARTENDER *My man!*

(MALCOLM continues to the back tables, where ADA, an ageing, good-natured whore, is sitting.)

ADA *I just knew my prayers was going to be answered. Because, I got a hole in my shoe, you know? and I just did not feel like tempting them nasty elements. Ain't them elements nasty?—And here you come, with your big handsome self, just like you knew how tired and thirsty your Ada was.—Sit down, sugar, and buy me a little sustenance.*

MALCOLM   *You better take your hands out of my waves,*
            you fool.

ADA   *Why, honey, I'll be glad to put the waves back in,*
        whenever you so desire.

MALCOLM   *Whenever I show desire—is that what you*
            said?

ADA   *Now, Red, you better talk respectful to me. I'm*
        mighty sensitive. And I carry a ice pick and a razor.

MALCOLM   *I see why you make out so well.*

    (The WAITRESS arrives to deliver MALCOLM's bour-
bon.)

ADA   *Honey, bring one of those for me.*

WAITRESS   *You ain't been drinking bourbon.*

ADA   *The gentleman will pay.*

WAITRESS   *The gentleman ain't said a word to me.*

ADA   *Impertinent peasant, I shall have you flogged.*

MALCOLM   *With her ice pick.—Go on, give Mama what*
            she wants.

WAITRESS   *Sugar, I don't know how you do it.*

ADA   *And I ain't about to tell you, neither. Then I'd be slinging and you'd be drinking.*

WAITRESS   *Oh, there's a little more to me than meets the eye.*

ADA   *Honey, I reckon that must be true.* (The WAITRESS, however, is now out of earshot.) *So, what's going down, sugar? How's Archie?*

MALCOLM   *Everything's pretty cool. Archie's okay.*

ADA   *I ain't seen him for several days.*

MALCOLM   *Well, you know Archie, baby.*

ADA   *Yeah, I reckon I do know the fool. Though I don't know why I call him a fool. I'm the fool.*

MALCOLM   *I don't know. I think things just happen to people. I don't think they even know themselves why what happens—happens.*

ADA   *I know. Nigger turned me around and I ain't been the same since.* (The WAITRESS arrives, with her bourbon.) *Thank you, sugar.* (To MALCOLM) *Bless you, Red. I got to go out in them elements in a minute. I just wanted to put it off.*

A GIRL'S VOICE OVER   *Hello, sugar. I'm sorry I'm late. But this rain—! nothing's moving!*

(MALCOLM's face changes, and he looks toward this voice.)

ADA   *You know her?*

MALCOLM   *How long she been coming around here?*

ADA   *Not long. A few weeks. Why?*

MALCOLM   *What's she doing?*

ADA   *She don't know yet. But she going to find out.*

DANIEL'S VOICE OVER   *—we got off the job early. So, I run home to change and I come straight here—*

GIRL'S VOICE OVER   *They didn't say nothing about this morning?*

DANIEL'S VOICE OVER   *What about this morning?*

(Close-up.)

LAURA   *Why, you were late—*

DANIEL   *Oh! Man needs me to keep his merchandise rolling, honey, he can't afford to give me but so much static. What you drinking?*

MALCOLM   *What does he do?*

ADA   *I don't believe he main-lining. Yet.*

(MALCOLM finishes his bourbon, puts money on the table.)

MALCOLM   *Well. I got to go out in them elements, too. Dig you later.*

ADA   *See you, Red. Remember what I said about me taking care of them waves.*

MALCOLM   *You ain't going to have me explaining to Archie how come you started running a barber shop!*

(ADA laughs.

MALCOLM walks slowly to the front of the bar. He stands there a moment.

LAURA is talking, very animatedly, to a young, good-looking, light-skinned boy—DANIEL. This is not quite the LAURA we saw earlier. She is still very, very young, but more sure of herself, freer—one may say, much happier.)

LAURA   *And then he made me type the letter over. And I had to smile at that no-good cracker real sweet, because, you know, they just found out that colored girls can type—that some colored girls can type—and I thought, oh, my Lord, don't this man know I got my baby uptown, wondering where his supper is, and I'm down here, making Metropolitan Life rich. Ain't a black man walking they ain't robbed blind. And I thought, Ain't that some shit!*

DANIEL   *I'm all right. I grabbed a sandwich.*

LAURA   *Oh, I'm going to take you home and feed you. You always been too skinny and you ain't really over that cold you caught last week.*

MALCOLM   *Excuse me, miss. Excuse me, sir. But ain't you Laura Blake, from Boston?*

(LAURA turns. She is holding a cigarette when she turns, and this cigarette somehow emphasizes her youth and the beautiful, total vulnerability of her face.)

LAURA   *Malcolm. Malcolm Little. My God. I heard you were in New York, but I never thought I'd see you here. It's so big.*

MALCOLM *It ain't so big. It just likes to act big. How you been?*

LAURA *I've been just fine. Though I don't think that question could have cost you many sleepless nights. How are you? You a lawyer yet?*

MALCOLM *No. Not yet.*

LAURA *Daniel, I want you to meet an old friend of mine, from Boston. We used to go dancing together. At the Roseland. Remember?—Daniel, this is Malcolm, Malcolm, this is Daniel.*

(The two dislike each other at once.)

DANIEL *How do you do?*

MALCOLM *Just fine. How are you?*

DANIEL *I can't complain. Laura—*

MALCOLM *You got time to have a quick drink with me? for old times' sake.*

LAURA *Old times—Daniel—?*

DANIEL *If your friend's buying—*

MALCOLM   *I'm buying—*

DANIEL   *—but, then, we have to run. I don't want to be late again tomorrow.*

MALCOLM   *I can understand that. What's your racket, friend?*

DANIEL   *Oh, I'm in charge of the shipping department of a clothing manufacturer downtown—*

LAURA   *It's a very responsible job.*

MALCOLM   *Well, we'll make it quick, then. Laura, what you learned to drink since I last saw you?* (To DANIEL) *When I knew her, she didn't drink nothing stronger than root beer.*

DANIEL   *She still don't drink. She gets two rum cokes in her, and she don't really know where she is.*

LAURA   *Well. I know where you are. And that's what matters.*

(The BARTENDER sets them up.)

BARTENDER   *Double this time, Red, or single?*

MALCOLM   *Better make it short, my friends is got to run.*

LAURA   *I got to fix supper. Daniel's hungry.*

MALCOLM   *How's your grandma?*

LAURA   *I haven't seen her, Malcolm, oh, for ages. I finally just had to get away from there, you know, it was driving me crazy. Just after you left—*

(DANIEL has swallowed his drink.)

DANIEL   *Laura—*

LAURA   *Yes, sugar?*

DANIEL   *You finish your drink with your friend. I'm going to go on to the house.*

LAURA   *But I'll come with you.*

DANIEL   *You ain't got to hurry. I'll just lie down. I don't feel too well.*

MALCOLM   *Don't let me keep you, Laura.*

DANIEL   *It's nothing. I'll be there.—Nice meeting you, man. Thanks.*

MALCOLM   *Nice meeting you.*

LAURA   *I'll be right home, Daniel.*

DANIEL   *Don't worry.—Bye!*

(He goes.)

LAURA   *He's restless, my man. Like you used to be.*

MALCOLM   *I'm still restless. I don't know if I've really changed much. But you've changed.*

LAURA   *How have I changed?*

MALCOLM   *I guess—you've kind of grown up—*

LAURA   *I had to try. I was such a stupid thing when you knew me. I've thought about it since—no wonder you ran!*

MALCOLM   *I didn't run from you. Not from you.*

LAURA   *Oh, it doesn't matter now. We were both kids then. And I guess we both had to find out things by ourselves. You were right about the hill. I could never have stayed there. But I didn't know I'd have to walk off of it—alone.*

MALCOLM   *Was it—very hard?*

LAURA   *It was a rather long walk.—I'd better go. Daniel worries when I'm late.*

MALCOLM   *You know him long?*

LAURA   *A few months. I met him—in the subway! Isn't that funny? I mean—for a girl like me?*

MALCOLM   *No. I don't think it's funny. Especially for a girl like you.*

LAURA   *What do you mean: especially?*

MALCOLM   *You always had a lot of life to you, somehow. You always wanted to live.*

LAURA   *If I don't get home and get supper on that table, my life may be in danger.—Do you come here often?*

MALCOLM   *Sometimes.—Do you?*

LAURA   *Sometimes.*

MALCOLM   *I've got to go, too. I'll walk out with you.*

(MALCOLM pays. LAURA adjusts her raincape.)

BARTENDER   *Thanks, Red. Goodnight.*

MALCOLM   *Goodnight.*

LAURA   *Goodnight!* (MALCOLM and LAURA walk into the rainy streets.) *Well—I go this way. It was nice seeing you, Malcolm.*

MALCOLM   *It was nice seeing you. Goodnight.*

LAURA   *Goodnight.*

(She starts away.)

MALCOLM   *Take care of yourself!*

LAURA   *I will, don't worry! Goodnight!*

(She runs up the avenue, like a little girl.

As she disappears, one of the syrupy, soupy ballads of the era begins to be heard—very much white folks' music.)

(In a darkened room, a radio is playing, very softly.

We slowly become aware of other sounds, the sounds of lovemaking, in fact.

SOPHIA's blond hair gleams on a pillow.

MALCOLM covers her.

We are aware, intermittently, throughout the following, of relentlessly cheerful American love songs, interspersed with commercials.

MALCOLM sits up and lights a cigarette. His face is angry and baffled.

SOPHIA kisses his arm, and he looks down at her.)

MALCOLM *You do this often?*

SOPHIA *What do you mean?*

MALCOLM *I mean, if you come to New York and you can't find me, do you just go out and pick up some other black stud? I mean, do you go around picking up black studs all the time?*

SOPHIA *Don't spoil it, Red.—Anyway, you aren't very black.*

MALCOLM *Don't tell me how black I am—I just asked a question. And I always distrust a person who's afraid to answer a question.*

SOPHIA *Red, what's the matter? You called me—you asked me to come.—I'd do anything for you. You know that.*

MALCOLM *We going to see about that. But what's your husband going to say?*

SOPHIA *I'm not married.*

MALCOLM *But you about to be married. That's what
you told me, little while ago. Reckon you better—a
fine, rich Boston chick like you. What he going to
say? that half-assed white boy you jerking off in the
back of a car because he don't want to defile your
body before the wedding.*

SOPHIA *Shut up. It's not like that at all.*

MALCOLM *Is it like it is with me?—One thing. Don't
ever tell me to shut up. You liable to find yourself
picking up teeth. You understand that?* (SOPHIA is
silent.) *You understand that?* (He slaps her.) *Now,
do you understand?*

SOPHIA (begins to weep) *Take your hands off me. I'm
going to get out of here.*

MALCOLM *You don't want to go nowhere. You ain't
really got no place to go. And if you go, you going
to come right back. We both know that.*

(LAURA and MALCOLM, running along the sand, falling down, laughing, at the water's edge.)

*Come on. Tell me about you and your white boy.
You love him?*

SOPHIA   *Of course I love him.*

MALCOLM   *As much as you love me?*

SOPHIA   *It's different. It's not the same. A person can love different people— differently.*

MALCOLM   *It's different, all right. You going to be married to him and putting out for me. Ain't that right? Answer me, bitch.*

SOPHIA   *Red. Don't do this to me. Please.*

MALCOLM   *What am I doing? All I'm doing is asking you to tell me the truth. Ain't nobody never asked you to tell the truth before?*

SOPHIA   *Look. We've had wonderful times with each other. And we still can. Nothing will change. We both know the score. I can't marry you. You don't want to marry me.*

MALCOLM   *That's the truest thing you ever said.*

SOPHIA   *It's not our fault the world is so fucked up. Maybe you think I'm an awful person—but, at least, I've never lied to you. If I have to live a certain kind of life in Boston, well, maybe that helps to protect us—look: the world sees a girl like me in a certain way. And if you give the world what it wants to see, then it stops looking. It doesn't look any further. And then—you're—free.*

MALCOLM *And so, instead of getting your little sister to cover for you, you can come to New York to go shopping—*

SOPHIA *I can come to New York to go shopping, to see friends, to go to the theater, to open charity balls, to do anything I want!*

MALCOLM *As a married woman.*

SOPHIA *Yes.*

MALCOLM *You something. What about him?*

SOPHIA *He'll never know. I'll keep him perfectly happy.*

MALCOLM *And me, too?*

SOPHIA *Yes.—If the world wasn't so fucked up—I wouldn't need him, for anything.*

(MALCOLM *grabs her roughly and kisses her—a long, brutal kiss. Then he pulls back and looks at her— proud, boyish, baffled, and evil.*)

MALCOLM *So you still my woman?*

SOPHIA *Yes. Always.*

MALCOLM (laughs) *Believe I'll put you on the block.*
   (SOPHIA begins kissing his neck, his chest. His
   hands tighten in her hair.) *Go on. Wish your white
   boy could see you now.*

   (Day. ARCHIE and MALCOLM, in MALCOLM's room.
They are sitting at a table; there is an envelope between
them.)

ARCHIE *Well. These greetings going to carry you away
   from here for a while.*

MALCOLM *They ain't going to carry me away. Not un-
   less I join the Japanese army.*

ARCHIE *Don't say that in public. They got spies, you
   know.*

MALCOLM *Spies? for the Japanese?*

ARCHIE *No. For us.*

MALCOLM *For us—?* (Thinking:) *They got spies
   watching—and listening—to us?*

87

(Day. MALCOLM before the Army psychiatrist: a studious young white man.)

MALCOLM   *How did you hear that I wanted to join the Japanese Army?—No. Wait a minute.*

(Puts his fingers to his lips, tiptoes to the door, and listens.

He then opens every closet door, ending with the door to the toilet—and disappears into the toilet for a moment, leaving the door open.

Then he returns to the PSYCHIATRIST, who is definitely intrigued.)

Listen. That Japanese talk didn't MEAN NOTH-ING. You from the North, man, ain't you?—like me. I'm sure you from the North, because I can smell a redneck. I mean, I can smell them! Now, you know what we going to do when I get in this man's uniform and go South? We going to start organizing, you dig me? Organizing, man, organize every nigger in this man's army and blow them crackers' heads off, like we should of done a long time ago, and you know it as well as me. That's what I'm talking about! Just let me get a gun in my hands, man, and the North don't have to worry about the South no more!

(ARCHIE is laughing so hard that he is crying. He,

and SOPHIA, and MALCOLM are seated at a table at Small's.)

PSYCHIATRIST   *Well, thank you for being so candid, Mr. Little. I'll make out my report, and—uh—you should be hearing from us soon.*

MALCOLM   *All* reet, *Daddy-o! I knew you'd dig it.— You try to hurry it up a little bit for me, okay?*

(MALCOLM shows ARCHIE his draft classification.)

ARCHIE   *Four-F. That's a good one, boy.*

SOPHIA   *You don't think they'll bother you again?*

MALCOLM   *You think they want to start the Civil War again?*

SOPHIA   *When Johnny comes marching home again—*

ARCHIE and MALCOLM   *Hurrah! Hurrah!*

SOPHIA   *We'll give him a hearty welcome then—*

ARCHIE and MALCOLM   *Hurrah! Hurrah!*

(This theme continues, musically, as we enter the dark streets of Harlem.

We pause at every mailbox.

Some of the Harlem citizens we have seen before, reading their mail: in a profound, silent, bitter melancholy.)

MALCOLM'S VOICE OVER   *Shit! You think I was about to fight in this man's army? This man who's killing me in* his *uniform, in* my *country, where I was born? We don't get killed facing the enemy—we get killed facing* him!

(At night: a group of young black soldiers, on 125th Street, some with girls, some finding girls, loud, good-natured, laughing—desperately, and briefly, free.

The rather nervous police—some on horseback.

We follow a black soldier and his girl. They are both a little drunk. They are both laughing.

The girl and the soldier disappear into a hotel.

The street down which we have followed them is quite dark and nearly deserted. We hear music from the neighboring bars, and voices, laughing and calling.

We remain in front of the hotel.

We hear a pistol shot.

The music continues, but the voices cease.)

WOMAN'S VOICE OVER   *Now, why'd you have to shoot him?*

(Her tone is exasperated: her question reasonable. People at the windows.

People on the fire escapes.

Children at the windows.

People on the stoops.

Children in the streets.

The voices of women, calling their children.

Swiftly: the faces of many children.

Children being hurried indoors, being hurried up the steps, and thrown into bed; windows being slammed, locked from the inside.

Doors being locked from the inside.

A policeman's horse, rearing.

Three golden balls outside a pawnbroker's shop.

A tenement window, with rags, or paper, stuffed in the jagged, broken glass.

A plate-glass window.

The tenement window.

The objects in the plate-glass window.

The tenement window.

The plate-glass window.

The plate-glass window is smashed.

Then, another. Then, another.

The hooves of rearing horses.

Garbage cans, rocks, bricks, indescribable debris, fill the screen.

The heads of horses, moving in.

The faces of people, grabbing, through the plate-glass windows, whatever can be carried.

The Chinese restaurant, with the sign, "Me Colored Too."

Clubs, rising and falling.

The people, surging, shouting.

Badges. Holsters. Sirens. Lights.

A sound truck, moving, voices appealing to the people to go home.

A black boy, running with more than he can carry.

He drops an overcoat.

An old woman, in a window, sees this.

She tells the young boy in the window next to her that the coat is just his size.

The boy runs down the stairs and into the streets, and swoops up the coat.

We follow him—or the coat—back up the narrow stairs.

Clubs against flesh; and

The boy trying on the coat before the old lady; and

A pistol being fired into the air; and

Someone going under beneath a club, or a hoof; and

The proud boy, turning in the overcoat.

Dawn. Silence. Devastation.)

(MALCOLM, in his room, rolling reefers. When he has about fifty sticks, he puts them in a Red Cross bandage box. He puts this box on a table.

From a drawer, he takes out a .25 automatic. He puts this under his belt, in the center of his back.

He sniffs some cocaine. Then he puts on his jacket, or his coat, placing the box of reefers under his armpit.

With his arm close to his side, he goes down into the street, to sell his wares.

We move along these streets at MALCOLM's pace, and see them from MALCOLM's point of view—perhaps slightly distorted, because MALCOLM is high.

Children, playing in the streets.

"Do-rag" brothers, quarreling and gambling on the stoops.

A young junkie, nodding.

Men and women, in front of a barber shop, or a bar.

An occasional, "Hey, Red!"

MALCOLM realizes that he is being shadowed.

He quickens his pace, and turns a corner, quickly.

He lets the Red Cross box fall into the gutter, and keeps walking.

He turns into a bar. This bar is not empty; not crowded.)

MALCOLM   *Bourbon and water, please.*

(The BARTENDER has the bottle poised over MALCOLM's glass, when two white PLAINCLOTHES MEN enter the bar.

The BARTENDER looks at the PLAINCLOTHES MEN, looks at MALCOLM. As they approach MALCOLM, he deliberately serves MALCOLM's drink, puts the bottle on the bar, and waits.

One of the PLAINCLOTHES MEN flashes his badge.)

PLAINCLOTHES MAN *You want to give it up, or you want us to take it? Because we know you got it.*

MALCOLM (loud) *You know I got what?*

PLAINCLOTHES MAN *Come on. Why don't you make it easy on yourself?*

MALCOLM (loud) *What the fuck you talking about, man?*

PLAINCLOTHES MAN *We'll ask the questions. That's what we get paid for.*

MALCOLM *Ain't you chumps got nothing better to do than follow black people around?—Here! I'm clean. I ain't got nothing on me. Nothing!* (To the bar, and especially to the BARTENDER.) *You all watch close, and make sure he don't plant nothing on me. You all know these dirty, white, low-life motherfuckers—they'd sell their own children for a stick of chewing gum!*

(The bar, and especially the BARTENDER, although silently, agree wholeheartedly with this sentiment. They watch the PLAINCLOTHES MEN with a silent, concentrated hatred, which is not without its effect on the hands of the one who is searching MALCOLM.)

94

PLAINCLOTHES MAN   *Turn out your pockets.* (Some of the people at the bar move a little closer to MAL-COLM.) *Stand back, can't you? We're not doing this for our health, you know.*

AN OLDER WOMAN   *I'm glad you know that much, you low-down, dirty dogs. And I wish I was your doctor. I'd take care of your* health.

(The BARTENDER, impassively, unobtrusively, moves in the direction of this lady, and serves her a drink.)

PLAINCLOTHES MAN   *Okay. You got us this time.*

MALCOLM   *I got you this time? What the fuck you talking about? You the ones been chasing me—and I always been clean, and you know it!*

PLAINCLOTHES MAN   *You may not be so lucky next time.*

MALCOLM   You *may not be so lucky next time.*

OLDER WOMAN   *Let the church say Amen!*

(The PLAINCLOTHES MEN exit.)

BARTENDER   *Let* us *ask the questions. That's what we get paid for. Shit. I know what them cocksuckers get paid for, and they ain't as good at it as their mamas is.* (Holding the bottle: to MALCOLM.) *Drink up, man. This here's on me.*

(Night. MALCOLM, carefully, enters his room: which has been searched.

MALCOLM realizes this at once.

Without seeming to reflect, he sniffs some cocaine.

Without seeming to reflect, he packs, and leaves.

In a swift montage, we see this happening two or three times.

Close-up: ARCHIE.)

ARCHIE *Red, I warned you, just as soon as that riot hit, this town would close up tighter than a virgin's asshole. And, boy, you ain't got that much Vaseline—! ain't nobody got it!*

(Close-up.)

MALCOLM *Yeah. I dig what you mean. It's tight, all right.*

MALCOLM'S VOICE OVER *Don't be telling me how much Vaseline I got, old man. I know I got more than you.*

(Close-up.)

ARCHIE *Lie low, let it blow over. All they doing is*

pruning the tree. That way, more apples going to
fall into fewer hands.

MALCOLM   *I dig.*

MALCOLM'S VOICE OVER   *You damn right, they going to*
fall into fewer hands.

(Close-up.)

ARCHIE   *Well. Guess I be getting on in. Ada be cooking*
supper, wondering where I am.

(Close-up.)

MALCOLM   *Yeah. I got a little run to make my own self.*
Say hello to old Ada for me.

MALCOLM'S VOICE OVER   *Old Ada is right. Two broken-*
down hustlers. Shit.

(Blows his nose, wipes his eyes; sniffs some more
cocaine.)

(Night. Sirens screaming.
We are someplace like New Jersey, or upper New
York State.
A patrol car, speeding.
MALCOLM, running, through back streets and alleys.

He slows to a walk, calculating the approach to an intersection.

We are in a white neighborhood.

MALCOLM steps off the curb, into the street, to halt a speeding patrol car.

He walks toward the car. We see him from the point of view of the patrolmen, as they rush toward him and grind the car to a halt.)

PATROLMAN   *Yeah, boy, what is it?*

MALCOLM   *Excuse me, policemens, I know you busy but I'm new in town and I wonder if you could kindly direct me to—*

PATROLMAN   *Get the fuck out of here, you stupid nigger!*

(And the car roars off.

MALCOLM watches the car disappear, with a remarkable, a dreadful expression on his face: pain, contempt, and pride. Then he laughs. Touches his pockets. Walks.)

(Night. A white carnation: in MALCOLM's lapel.

He is standing outside the Astor Hotel, at 45th and Broadway, watching the traffic.

A car, driven by a pale, obviously wealthy white man, about sixty, slows at the curb, and MALCOLM gets in.

The WHITE MAN moves over, and MALCOLM takes the wheel.

They drive in silence. The white man is obviously under great pressure. When they arrive in Harlem, this pressure—some strange delight—seems to become almost unbearable.

MALCOLM gives the white man a wry, amused glance.

They stop in front of a Harlem building. The WHITE MAN furtively slips into the building.

MALCOLM follows him. They climb the stairs.

They knock on a door which opens to reveal a very beautiful, hard, black girl—very black. She is obviously naked under her robe.

She winks at MALCOLM, then fixes the WHITE MAN with a hard, cruel look.

The WHITE MAN, beginning to tremble, places some money in MALCOLM's hands.)

WHITE MAN   *I'll give you double—if you stay, and
    watch.*

THE GIRL   *Come on in.* (She closes the door behind
    them. Close-up: MALCOLM's unbelieving and horri-
    fied face.)

GIRL'S VOICE OVER   *Now, what you come back here for,
    you low-down, dirty, white scum-bag? Didn't I tell
    you what I'd do to you if I ever caught you round*

here again? I guess you didn't believe me, did you?
Well, do you believe this? (The sound of a blow.)
Take off them clothes, you faggot! Take them off!
I ain't going to tell you twice—(The sound of several blows in succession; a sound of whimpering.)
Oh. You going to get it tonight.

WHITE MAN'S VOICE OVER   *Oh. Please. Please. I know I deserve it. Oh. Please. Please.* (The WHITE MAN's shirt, tie, trousers, shoes, are scattered violently about the room.) *Is he watching? Oh, watch. Watch. Please.*

GIRL'S VOICE OVER   *He's watching.* (The whip whistles through the air.) *We going give him a show.*

WHITE MAN'S VOICE OVER   *Oh, watch, watch. Please. Harder. Harder. Blacker.*

(MALCOLM, at the wheel of another car, conducting a party of half a dozen people, white, male and female, up to Harlem.

The door is answered by a handsome, elegantly dressed, brown-skinned matron.

As the party files in, we move ahead of them and discover, sitting on a great bed, a naked black man and a naked white woman.

We watch the white faces watching them.

The brown-skinned matron's cruelly contemptuous face.

She looks at MALCOLM and they each, nearly imperceptibly, shrug.)

(Night. MALCOLM, tossing and dreaming.

The figures in his dream are superimposed on his tormented, wet face. The elegant brown-skinned matron seems to have become his mother. She raises the whip, smiling. She brings the whip down on the shoulders of a naked black man. But this black man has his father's face. MALCOLM hears snatches of his father's song. Then the whip is in a white girl's hands, and it is SOPHIA who rakes the whip across MALCOLM's face. MALCOLM screams, and grabs the whip. He wraps his fingers in SOPHIA's blond hair and raises the butt of the whip to strike her. Her face turns into LAURA's face.

MALCOLM wakes up.

He reaches for the cocaine on the night table, sniffs, turns back into sleep.

Morning. MALCOLM, mechanically, sniffs cocaine, gets out of bed, begins to get dressed.)

(Night. A Billie Holiday type singer, in a 52nd Street joint, singing the blues.

A high, exuberant MALCOLM, digging this: with SOPHIA and ARCHIE.

The song ends. They applaud. MALCOLM leans over and kisses SOPHIA lightly.)

SOPHIA (to ARCHIE)   *He ought to hit the number every
    day.*

ARCHIE   *For three hundred bucks? Shit, I'd soon be out
    of business.*

MALCOLM   *Daddy-o, you got to take the rough with
    the smooth, the bitter with the sweet, you told me
    that yourself, Papa! Now, you just sit up and let
    Brother Malcolm pour you another little taste of
    this here*—(Reaches for the bottle on the table,
    pours. The music begins again. Lowering his
    voice.)—*because I remember everything you ever
    told me, baby. And I'm mighty grateful to you.*

ARCHIE (to SOPHIE: dry)   *Maybe you right.*

(And they listen to the music.)

(Morning. MALCOLM and SOPHIA, in bed, sleeping.
There is a knocking at the door.
    MALCOLM, automatically — half asleep — slides
what's left of his cocaine, which is on a round, two-
sided shaving mirror, under the bed.)

MALCOLM   *Who is it?*

ARCHIE'S VOICE   *It's me, Red. Archie.*

(MALCOLM looks at the clock. It's early—looks at
SOPHIA, who has come awake; and gets out of bed.)

MALCOLM *I'm coming.* (He stumbles to the door and
    opens it. ARCHIE stands there, with a gun leveled at
    MALCOLM.) *Man—!*

ARCHIE *I keep my figures in my head, Red. But, every
    once in a while, I write some numbers down when
    I get home, just to double-check myself. And, Red,
    you lied. About that number. That weren't no hit.*

(MALCOLM, in his comatose state, is having great
trouble digesting all of this.)

MALCOLM *Come on in the house, man. Put that thing
    away.*

ARCHIE *I ain't coming in this house. Your chick in there
    with you, ain't she? I don't want no witnesses.*

MALCOLM *Archie, she was there when you paid me,
    when I told you the number, and you paid me!*

ARCHIE *Yeah. I know she'll swear to it.*

MALCOLM *Archie—I swear to God, man!*

(We realize that MALCOLM's voice is beginning to wake up other people.)

ARCHIE (lightly touches him with the gun) *You got until noon tomorrow to give me back the three hundred dollars you stole. And I'm giving you a break. Because I know what you thinking. You think I'm old and I ain't worth shit and I ain't got it no more. You think you got it. Well, you ain't got it yet, baby. You still got to get it from me.* (Puts away his gun, walks away.) *Till noon tomorrow, baby!*

MALCOLM *Where, sir?*

ARCHIE *Where the fuck you think! In the middle of Times Square! I'll be wearing dark glasses and holding a cup!*

(This increases the storm of neighborly protest. MALCOLM slowly closes the door.)

SOPHIA *Red—*

MALCOLM *Hold it, honey. Just hold it a minute.*

(He sits down on the bed.)

SOPHIA *I was there when you played the number. I was*

*there when he paid you—Archie's never made a
mistake like this before!*

MALCOLM   *That may be true. But, right now, I swear
I don't remember what number I played.*

SOPHIA   *You combinated 598. I remember.*

MALCOLM   *I'm sure you right. But—that don't make no
difference, neither. (Smiles.) I swear, this must be
one of the few times in history that a white woman's
word don't mean shit.*

SOPHIA   *Well. Then, let's just pay him his three hundred
dollars.*

(MALCOLM turns to her, exasperated; then, he
smiles.)

MALCOLM   *Honey, I know you mean well. But I can't
do that—you don't see that, do you?*

SOPHIA   *No. I don't.*

MALCOLM   *I didn't think you would, somehow—*

SOPHIA   *I don't care about the money, and you can always pay me back!*

MALCOLM   *But I can't pay Archie back, little girl. You
think he come here, with that gun, to talk about
money?*

SOPHIA   *That's all I heard him talk about.*

MALCOLM   *But it ain't all I heard him talk about. Shit,
if Archie thought I needed money, he'd hustle up
three hundred, six thousand dollars—! I can't pay
him because I swear I didn't cheat him, so if I pay
him, I'm a pussy. You know the life expectancy for
pussy out here? And if Archie don't make me pay
him, you can just sweep him away and forget it—
he'd be worse than a pussy, because he's getting
old now and young cats like me is on his ass because
he been out here too long. Ain't no retirement age
out here. You don't get no pension. No social se-
curity benefits, baby—sad, ain't it?*

SOPHIA   *Red. What are you going to do?*

MALCOLM   *Well, the first thing I'm going to do is get
your ass up off that bed and into the first thing smoking, back to Boston.*

SOPHIA   *Why?*

MALCOLM   *Because you're going to be in the way here,*

that's why. Now, don't give me no shit, get up and get dressed and get out of here.

SOPHIA   *Red—*

MALCOLM   *I don't want you to get hurt, baby. Now, move your ass.*

(Day. SOPHIA, dressed, and at the door. She gives him nearly all the money in her purse.)

SOPHIA   *Here. I just need taxi fare when I get to Boston.*

MALCOLM   *Okay. See you.*

SOPHIA   *You want me to send Shorty down?*

MALCOLM   *I don't want you to do nothing but get out of here! Go on, now— I'll call you.*

SOPHIA   *Okay, Red.*

(She kisses him, lightly, goes.

When the door closes behind SOPHIA, MALCOLM carefully locks it, goes to the window, looks out into the streets.

We see SOPHIA, with her traveling bag, slowly leave the building and slowly cross the street. A cab comes along, she hails it, gets in, and is carried away.

Then, the streets seem empty and ominous.

MALCOLM recovers his cocaine, gets himself high. He finishes dressing, puts his gun under his belt—in front, against his ribs, this time—and goes out into the streets.

He enters the bar in which we watched the encounter with the two PLAINCLOTHES MEN.

The BARTENDER pours him a drink the moment he sees him.)

BARTENDER   *If you ever been cool, be cool today.*

MALCOLM   *Dad?*

BARTENDER   *Every chump, and his mama*—plus *the heat.*

MALCOLM   *Who's selling tickets?*

BARTENDER   *I got the hot dog concession, myself.*

MALCOLM   *Some shit—!*

(Turns to go.)

BARTENDER   *If you need me—*

MALCOLM   *I'm cool.* (He steps into the street. The moment he does, a young BOY steps up to him, whispers

something in his ear, steps back, laughing. MAL-
COLM stares at the BOY, speechless.) *Say that again,
son?*

BOY   *I said, I hear you take it—*

(MALCOLM strikes the BOY with a kind of accumula-
tion of rage, strikes him before he thinks.

The BOY has been ready for this, and wades in.

MALCOLM is a very able street-fighter, but the BOY is,
too; and the BOY is younger, and MALCOLM is high.

People gather to watch, some would like to separate
them.

The battle does not last long. MALCOLM goes down.

The BOY laughs, walks slowly away.

The BARTENDER comes out, and leads MALCOLM into
the bar.)

BARTENDER   *If you got anything, give it to me—quick!*

(MALCOLM gives him his gun, slumps down on the
barstool.

The BARTENDER stashes the gun behind the bar.

He has scarcely done this when a white COP enters,
his hand on his gun butt.)

COP   *Red. Stand up. Take that hand out of your pocket.
Real carefully.*

(MALCOLM does this. The COP leads him out into the
street, to his partner, next to the patrol car; which is
doubleparked, with its radio going.

People gather to watch, as MALCOLM is frisked; and
this is even more humiliating for him than the battle
with the BOY.)

COP   *We had a reliable report, Red, that you would be
sure to be carrying a gun today.*

MALCOLM   *I had one. But I threw it in the river.*

(They watch each other. On the COP's face is a certain, wry pity.)

COP   *Well, try not to join it.* (Gets into his car. Looks
out.) *I think it's about time you left town, Red.*

(The patrol car drives away.

MALCOLM stands watching it, then becomes aware
of the people watching him; he reenters the bar.

He takes his gun back from the BARTENDER, and
sits down.)

BARTENDER   *What are you going to do?*

MALCOLM   *I don't know.*

(He puts his head in his hands.)

OSTROVSKI'S VOICE OVER (loud) —*something a colored person can do*—(MALCOLM looks around the bar, slowly: we see the people from his point of view, and as he sees them: aimless, lost, without hope.) *Something a colored person can do!*

LAURA'S VOICE OVER *Why—you—you could be great! You could be a wonderful man, Malcolm!*

LAURA'S VOICE OVER *You a lawyer yet?*

MALCOLM'S VOICE OVER *No. Not yet.*

OSTROVSKI'S VOICE OVER *Something a colored person can do!*

(Night. MALCOLM appears not to have moved.
He signals for a drink.
MALCOLM's back is now to the camera.
The BARTENDER serves the drink, looks straight ahead, over MALCOLM's shoulder, and stiffens.
MALCOLM slowly turns: to face ARCHIE, and ARCHIE's gun.
ARCHIE is very high.)

ARCHIE *I told you I meant business, Red.*

(The bar is frozen, watching them.

MALCOLM says nothing. He does not dare take his eyes off ARCHIE.)

ARCHIE   *I know what you thinking. But nobody makes a chump out of West Indian Archie—nobody! I been out here too long. I taught you everything you know. How come you to think that you could fuck with me, boy? Was it because I trusted you?*

MALCOLM   *Archie—*

ARCHIE   *I know what you thinking. You thinking, I'm a old man now, and you sitting there, just waiting to get the jump on me. But it ain't going to happen. I'll tell you why it ain't going to happen. It ain't going to happen, because the moment you move, you dead. I don't care. I done already been to Sing Sing. I done already served some time, so I don't care. But, if you plug me, which, like I say, it ain't too fucking likely, you going serve some time. And then—you be just like me.*

(We see that MALCOLM knows that this is true. The BARTENDER comes from behind the bar.)

BARTENDER   *Archie, give the kid a break. Red was like a son to you. You don't want to hurt him. I know*

112

you don't want to hurt him.—Won't nobody think it's because you're scared.—Archie?

A WOMAN *He right, Archie. We can't start killing our own children.*

A MAN *Let the white folks do that, Archie.*

BARTENDER *Come in the back and sit down. Come on.*

(They, slowly, lead ARCHIE away.

MALCOLM sits perfectly still. There is a great space around him. No one comes near him.

Finally, he drops a bill on the bar, and rises, and walks out into the street. He stands outside the bar for a long time, waiting.

Then, he turns and walks slowly away.

We see SHORTY, driving slowly through Harlem.

We see the streets from SHORTY's point of view. It is that hour when the bars are just beginning to empty.

From quite far away, we see MALCOLM, walking.

SHORTY begins honking his horn, speeds up.

MALCOLM's weary, high face.

The honking of the horn slowly begins to penetrate his consciousness.

SHORTY speeds up, and honks more insistently.

MALCOLM's eyes grow wide with the fear of death. He draws his gun, and turns.)

SHORTY (shouts) *Homeboy!*

>   (He stops the car, and jumps out.
>   MALCOLM falls into his arms.)

>   (Morning. Boston. MALCOLM, asleep. SOPHIA watching him. Day. MALCOLM, walking, alone, through Boston —the route which we have previously traversed with SHORTY.
>   Day. SHORTY's apartment.
>   SHORTY, SOPHIA, a young mulatto of Italian extraction, RUDY, and MALCOLM.
>   MALCOLM is seated on the bed. The group is gathered around him.
>   A meeting is just ending.)

MALCOLM   *Okay. The first heist, tomorrow night, up at Rudy's faggot's house. That'll be real short and sweet. Sophia's already cased us a couple of other joints, and she's going to be visiting more. Okay. We all know what we got to do. But there's one more thing.* (He looks around at all their faces.) *We all responsible for each other now, is that right?* (They nod.) *But I'm your chief, so I'm responsible for all of you. Right?* (They nod again.) *Let me show you something.*

>   (He takes out his revolver, and drops one bullet into it.

They watch him.

He looks up, smiles, puts the revolver to his head, and pulls the trigger.

SOPHIA screams.

SHORTY reaches out, but MALCOLM points the revolver at him. SHORTY moves back.)

SHORTY *What are you doing, man!*

(MALCOLM again puts the revolver to his head, and pulls the trigger.

SOPHIA begins to cry.)

SHORTY *Please, man!*

(MALCOLM puts the revolver to his head, and pulls the trigger once more. Then he looks up into their desperate faces.)

MALCOLM *Now. Remember: I did that to let you know I'm not afraid to die. I know all of you have better sense than to mess with a man who's not afraid to die.—Now, get out of here, all of you, and let me get myself straight.*

(Shaken and speechless, they slowly leave.

When they have left, we see that MALCOLM had palmed the bullet: the revolver had been empty.

MALCOLM loads the revolver, and laughs.)

SOPHIA'S VOICE OVER   *There's nothing in the basement,*
   so forget that—(SOPHIA's hand, drawing a map of a
   house. The others are watching intently.)—*the safe*
   is in the library, just behind *the bookshelf—in fact,*
   just behind Charles Dickens—the easiest way to get
   at it—

(We see a swift montage of SOPHIA, sipping tea at
some very elegant house, RUDY, catering at some very
posh party, and, over this, simultaneously, SOPHIA's
hand, or RUDY's hand, drawing maps of houses.

   The entire gang, at a nightclub, dressed to kill: having a high old time, seen through the paper on which the
hand inexorably draws maps of houses.

   MALCOLM, smoking reefers; sniffing cocaine; stoned
out of his head.

   Night. Rain. RUDY, sitting in the get-away car, outside a Boston mansion.

   A finger-beam searchlight, inside the house.

   SHORTY and MALCOLM, operating with a silent effi-
ciency.

   They get the loot into the car. The back seat looks
like a pawnshop.

   MALCOLM gets in last, he, SHORTY, and RUDY, in the
front seat, and they drive off.

   From RUDY's point of view, we see a police car turn
the corner, driving toward them.)

MALCOLM   *Be cool.* (They continue driving. The police

car passes them. MALCOLM, watching the rear-view mirror. The rear-view mirror: in which we see the police car stop and make a U-turn, driving back toward them.) *Stop the car.*

RUDY *Are you crazy?*

MALCOLM *Stop the car.* (MALCOLM takes a piece of paper out of his pocket, and gets out of the car. He hails the police car—which has just begun to flash its lights—and stops it.) *Excuse me, policemens, I know you busy. But we just got here, sir, and I wonder if you could direct me to this address.* (Hands the piece of paper to the POLICEMEN, looking very worried.)

POLICEMAN *Yeah. Go straight ahead. Take your first left till you get to the second stoplight. You turn right—and you'll be close to home.*

MALCOLM (takes the paper back) *Thank you, sir.* (He returns to the get-away car.) *Okay. Let's go.* (The police car makes a U-turn, and drives away.)

SHORTY *What did you do, man?*

MALCOLM *I gave them my address. And then I asked them if they could tell me how to get there.—And they told me. And I thanked them.*

117

(He laughs. SHORTY begins to laugh.

In a moment, they are all rocking with laughter.

A wristwatch, on MALCOLM's arm, filling the screen with ticking.

MALCOLM, in SHORTY's apartment, stoned out of his head, looks at the watch, turns over on his side again.

The watch: which stops ticking.

The watch: being handed back to MALCOLM, over the counter of a repair shop.

The watch: on MALCOLM's arm as he walks, ticking.

We walk behind MALCOLM as though we were following him and do not want to be seen.

We travel upstairs to the apartment.

MALCOLM lays the watch on the dresser.

He takes off his shirt.

He looks into the mirror.

He sniffs a little cocaine.

He brushes his hair, preparing to conk it.

He massages the congolene into his hair.

We look both ways, up and down the wintry, deserted street.

We approach the house, very slowly.

We come slowly up the stairs.

MALCOLM's hand, turning the faucet.

The pipes make a choked, protesting sound, but there is no water.

We turn a landing and come up the stairs, toward MALCOLM's door.

The dry faucet. MALCOLM turns the other faucet: which is also dry.

He tries again: both faucets.

MALCOLM's sweating face, as the congolene begins to burn.

He rushes to the toilet bowl and pulls the chain and puts his head in the bowl.

The water splashes over his head.

Loud knocking at the door.

MALCOLM pulls the chain again. He has not heard the knocking: which has been drowned out for him by the roar of the water.

The knocking: louder.)

VOICE OVER   *Police! Open up! Open up in there!*

(MALCOLM, gasping. His hands reach for a towel.
Now, MALCOLM hears the knocking, and freezes.
The knocking is louder and louder and louder.
Close-up: MALCOLM, dripping, walking to the door.
The knocking of a judge's gavel.
Close-up: SOPHIA.)

JUDGE'S VOICE OVER   *—to the Framingham Reformatory for Women for a period of not less than one and not more than five years—*

(Close-up: SHORTY.)

JUDGE'S VOICE OVER *Count one, eight to ten years—*
count two, eight to ten years—(SHORTY begins to
tremble. Close-up: MALCOLM.)—*count three, eight*
to ten years—(We hear SHORTY begin to moan.)—
the sentences to run concurrently—

(We hear SHORTY scream.
But we remain on MALCOLM's proud, bitter, unutterably ruined and unutterably juvenile face: staring at
the JUDGE, with murder in his eyes.)

(Day. The license-plate shop, in the prison.

The men are quietly working.

A tremendous commotion is heard, and LUTHER, a big, black man in his late thirties, looks up toward the source of this commotion.

PETE, a younger prisoner, grins and shrugs.)

PETE   *It's Satan again.*

MALCOLM'S VOICE (shouting)   *I didn't do a damn thing! I was minding my own business when this joker come fucking with me! I ain't no punk!*

OTHER VOICES (ad-lib)   *Hold it! Hold it! Get him! Break the bastard's balls!*

(Close-up of LUTHER as he begins moving toward the fracas.

TWO GUARDS, with difficulty, separate MALCOLM *and* another inmate.)

FIRST GUARD   *Hold your tongue, boy, everybody knows who's the troublemaker around here.*

MALCOLM   *Why you always take up for him? Because he lets you feel his ass all the time?*

(The SECOND GUARD knocks him down.)

MALCOLM (rising)   *It's because of all that good pussy he gives you, you dirty, depraved hyena—!*

(Both GUARDS are beating him mercilessly now, and dragging him away.)

PETE   *You're the hyena, you no-good, mariney bastard!*

LUTHER   *Shut up.*

MALCOLM'S VOICE   *I ain't got to fix my face to please you bastards, just because I'm in prison!*

(MALCOLM is dragged away. The door to the license-plate shop thunders behind them.)

PETE   *Well, what the hell makes him act like that? He been in trouble with everybody ever since he got here.*

(LUTHER looks at PETE—hard, as though he were looking at a peculiar kind of insect.)

LUTHER   *He don't dig being locked up. Now, most people, they* dig *being locked up. They really dig it. Makes things easier for them. Take you, for example. You going to make sure you stay locked up all your life. You wouldn't know what to do if you was free.*

122

(MALCOLM, still shouting, being kicked and punched into solitary.)

MALCOLM   *You ain't never going to make me eat your shit! Never! You dirty white motherfuckers!*

SECOND GUARD   *You'll be glad to eat shit by the time you get out of here, boy.*

(And a final blow hurls MALCOLM against the wall of the cell. He goes down. The GUARDS slam the door to the cell.
Close-up: MALCOLM as he painfully, slowly, pulls himself up against the wall.)

MALCOLM   *I hate every one of you—every one of you— and your dirty white God sitting in heaven on his white behind—and that cunt, the Virgin Mary, and that punk Jesus—and all the little white children— if I could—if I could—I'd beat your brains out and tear out your hearts—reach up your asses and tear out your guts with my hand—*

(He smashes his fist against the wall, grabs it in pain, and slumps, moaning.)

(Night. the prison cinema, which is showing a Humphrey Bogart movie. We hear snatches of the dialogue, and we hear pistol shots: the reaction of the black inmates is more sardonic than that of the whites.

We pan over the prisoners' faces, and come to rest on MALCOLM's bandaged fist.

MALCOLM attempts to light a cigarette. He cannot quite manage it.

A light is struck in the darkness next to him. MALCOLM looks up.

LUTHER holds the match and lights MALCOLM's cigarette.)

MALCOLM   *Thanks.*

LUTHER   *Don't believe everything you see in the movies. Only a white devil like Bogart can do everything with his fists.* (MALCOLM stares at him.) *We have to learn how to use our heads.*

(Close-up: MALCOLM, dimly pondering this, as his eyes return to the screen.)

(Day. The license-plate shop.

MALCOLM, working, and having trouble working because of his bandaged fist: in a surly, sullen silence.

LUTHER is working, and talking to a group of men.)

LUTHER   *The North ain't got no reason to talk about the South so bad. Were we in the South, we'd be out on the roads or in somebody's damn plantation, working to keep some peckerwood rich. We doing the same thing here. You ever figure out the profit somebody's making on these here license plates?*

HANK (a prisoner) *Shit. You being taught a useful trade.*

LUTHER *Oh. I know it's a useful trade. Ain't no doubt about that. But I don't want no peckerwood thinking that it's useful to me. He ain't got nothing that's useful to me.*

(A few of the MEN laugh; a few look around to see how the GUARDS are taking this.

MALCOLM is not a part of the group; he is listening but he does not react.)

FRANK (a prisoner) *You a bitch with your shit, Luther. But we in this white man's country. Now, what you fixing to do—? you fixing to start a new country?*

LUTHER *Yes.* (Laughter. LUTHER is unperturbed.) *The trouble with most black cats in this country is that they don't know what color they is.*

PETE *You talking about them real mariney cats?*

(MALCOLM stiffens, but does not turn around.)

LUTHER *No. I ain't especially talking about them. Shit,
I've known cats as black as my shoe, had to light a
match to find themselves when they looked into the
mirror, and the white man had them so brainwashed
they thought they was white. The white man's run a
hell of a game down on us—and we so stupid we
go for it.*

(Close-up: MALCOLM, smiling.
Close-up: a GUARD: not pleased.)

GUARD *You about to wind up your sermon for the day?*

LUTHER *No.—Most of them real light cats look that
way because some no-good white peckerwood raped
their grandmother.* (To the GUARD) *And they so
sick, they proud of that!*

(Evening. MALCOLM, in the shower, alone, luxuriat-
ing in the feel of the water against his skin, head down,
thinking.

We hear sounds of the other prisoners quite nearby.

MALCOLM turns off the shower, dries himself, ties a
towel around his waist, begins massaging his hair, pre-
paratory to giving it a new "conk."

LUTHER enters, watches MALCOLM for a moment.)

LUTHER *How you feeling, Red? Fist still giving you
trouble?*

MALCOLM   *It's better. How'd you know my name was Red?*

LUTHER   *It just figures.*

MALCOLM   *You the first person ever to call me by my name—in this joint.*

LUTHER   *I'm just more observant than they are.* (MALCOLM starts massaging in the Vaseline.) *Red, you got more sense than any cat in this prison—only, you don't use it. You ain't using your brains when you go around busting your fist against stone walls. That's just what the white man wants you to do. Like he wants us to keep fighting each other—because as long as we fighting each other, we ain't fighting him. And he wants you to beat your* brains out, *Red, against that stone wall he's built. That's why he built it—for you to beat your brains out against it.* (MALCOLM looks at him, still massaging his hair.) *Why do you do that, Red?*

MALCOLM   *Why do I do what?*

LUTHER   *Put all that poison in your hair?*

MALCOLM   *Everybody does. All the cats.*

LUTHER   *Yes. But why? Why does everybody do it?*

MALCOLM   *Well, hell, you don't want to walk around with your head all nappy, looking like—looking like—*

(He stops, staring at LUTHER.)

LUTHER   *Looking like what?—Looking like—me, for example? Looking like your father?*

MALCOLM   *Well—looking—like—*

LUTHER   *You don't want to look like what you are. What makes you ashamed of what you are?*

MALCOLM   *Look, man, I ain't said I was* ashamed—

LUTHER   *You go to all that trouble and all that pain and sweat and put all that poison in your hair, what for? Because you ashamed of being black and you want to be white.*

MALCOLM   *Oh, man, I don't want to hear all that—*

LUTHER   *I've seen you cats be-bopping down the avenue in your clown suits and with all that mess in your hair. You cats look like monkeys. The white man sees you and he laughs. He* laughs. *Because he knows you ain't white. But as long as you want to be white, he's got you where he wants you.* (MAL-

COLM says nothing.) *You've always been pretty proud of that light skin of yours, haven't you?*

MALCOLM *Oh—! I don't know if it's anything to be proud of—*

LUTHER *You heard me explaining the other day how come you got to be that color, didn't you?* (MALCOLM nods.) *What color is your father?*

(Close-up: MALCOLM, very moved.)

MALCOLM *My father was black.*

LUTHER *Is he still living?*

MALCOLM *No. My father's dead. My father was a follower of Marcus Garvey—and some white men killed him, when I was little.*

LUTHER *And you've spent your life trying to look like the man who raped your mother and murdered your father.*

(Close-up: MALCOLM. This thought has never crossed his mind before.
He is furious at LUTHER, and humiliated.)

LUTHER *And you got the nerve to call yourself a man.*

(They stare at each other.) *If you a man—a real man—you'll throw all that poison away. Right now.*

MALCOLM   *How come you to start messing in my business, man?* (But his tone is not convincing; LUTHER is not intimidated. MALCOLM looks helplessly at the Vaseline on his hands, slowly wipes them on the towel which drapes his loins.) *I mean—you don't bug none of the other prisoners.*

LUTHER   *They too far gone. But I got a message for you.* (Close-up: MALCOLM, wary.) *I can show you how to get out of prison.*

(Close-up: MALCOLM.
The words "out of prison!" resound through his skull, seem to bounce against the walls of the entire prison.)

MALCOLM   *How?*

(Close-up: LUTHER, calculating.
Close-up: MALCOLM, tense.
He shakily lights a cigarette.)

LUTHER   *First thing you got to do: you can't eat no more pork.*

(MALCOLM looks up, astounded.
Insert: LOUISE, in the asylum.)

LOUISE   *I said it, just as plain—don't let them feed that
boy no pig.*

(Close-up: MALCOLM, listening to LUTHER.)

LUTHER   *And another thing: when you finish that cigarette—don't smoke any more.*

(Close-up: MALCOLM looks wonderingly from the
cigarette to LUTHER.
Close-up: LUTHER.)

LUTHER   *And I'll show you how to get out of prison. I'll
show you how to be free.* (He turns to go, stops.)
*You know—when you get your freedom, you got to
know everything the white man knows. They got a
library in this prison. I'd start to using it, if I was
you.* (Starts to go, and again returns.) *And I'd take
that English correspondence course, if I was you.
You got to learn not to waste the time, Malcolm.
You got to learn how to use the time.*

(MALCOLM looks up at him.
Insert: EARL LITTLE's face.
Close-up: LUTHER.)

MALCOLM   *Yes.—Sir.*

(LUTHER goes.

MALCOLM sits in silence, thinking.

He looks at the empty cigarette pack. He slowly crumples it in his fist.

He looks at the burning cigarette.

He takes a last drag on it, then throws it away.)

(Night. MALCOLM's cell.

MALCOLM, awake, in his bunk.)

MALCOLM'S VOICE   *I wonder what kind of hype Luther's figured out. But Luther must know what he's talking about. He's been right about everything else. But how does it work? Is it like the hype I worked on the Army? Or does it do something to your body —or your mind—wow—maybe that's it—maybe it's a psychological hype—when you don't smoke cigarettes and don't eat pork? Especially when you always have. Shit. It must be something like that.— I know one thing. I'll do anything to get out of prison. Anything. Anything.*

(Day. The prison library.

Long shot. MALCOLM, gawky and frightened—the first time we have seen him overtly frightened since the conk scene—entering this library.

He begins walking toward us, examining the bookshelves.

He touches each book rather as though it were alive

and might touch him back—always coming closer and closer to us.

He picks up a book and puts it, distrustfully, under his arm.

Close-up: MALCOLM.

He opens the book again.

Reverse shot. Night. MALCOLM's cell.

We see that the book is the dictionary, and MALCOLM is muttering to himself the first word.

Close-up: the first word: "aardvark.")

MALCOLM's VOICE   *Aardvark.—A long-tailed, long-eared, burrowing African mammal.—Sounds like the dozens to me.—Lives off—termites?—I wonder what Luther's putting down.*

(Day. MALCOLM's cell.

A mimeographed list of books for the English correspondence course being handed into MALCOLM's hands.

Close-up: MALCOLM, studying this list, marking off the titles that appeal to him.

Close-up: the list, as MALCOLM writes his number against the books he wants.)

(Day. The prison lunch room. Crowded, noisy, vivid.

MALCOLM sits at the table among the men, silent, and very far away from them.

Traveling shot: the meat platter as it passes among the men, down the table.

Angle: the platter comes to MALCOLM.

He takes it, hesitates.

He seems suddenly to wake from a dream.

Close-up: MALCOLM.)

LUTHER'S VOICE (reverberating in his head) *Don't eat any more pork.*

(He passes the platter to the man next to him.

Angle, favoring the man next to MALCOLM.

The man next to MALCOLM starts to serve himself, then stops and looks at MALCOLM.

Angle, favoring MALCOLM.)

MALCOLM *I don't eat pork.*

(Traveling shot. Close. The platter continues down the table.

Pan: the astonished faces at the table, staring at MALCOLM.

Close-up: LUTHER's proud face.)

(Day. The prison yard.

Two shot. MALCOLM and LUTHER, walking.)

LUTHER *The first people ever created were black people. Black people. There wasn't a single white face*

to be found in all the universe. I can prove it. Every
scholar knows it. The white man's been lying to us
for all these thousands of years.

MALCOLM   *My father used to say that.*

LUTHER   *That's why he's dead. He was a bad nigger.*

(They walk out of the frame. The camera does not
move and the other prisoners, ab-libbing their various
preoccupations, walk into camera and out of the frame.
The population of the prison is two-thirds black.
Two shot. MALCOLM and LUTHER, walking.)

LUTHER   *They don't want black men to hear the truth.*
That's why any black man even tries to tell the truth
is murdered by these white devils. Why, if black
men knew the truth—! there'd be no black men in
this prison.

(Pan: the GUARDS.
Two shot. MALCOLM and LUTHER, walking.)

LUTHER   *We are a nation. A nation. But the white man*
don't want us to know that. He wants to make us be-
lieve that he's the only—nation!

(Pan: the black faces.
Two shot. MALCOLM and LUTHER.)

MALCOLM   *I don't know what you know. But I know you know something.*

LUTHER   *I know a black man sent by Allah to rescue this black nation. God is a man, Malcolm. A black man.—God is black.*

MALCOLM (laughs)   *God is—black?* (He touches, involuntarily, his face.) *God is—black?*

LOUISE'S VOICE   *Go stand in the sun and get some color, boy.*

VOICE OF THE YOUNG MALCOLM   *Mama, are you white?*

LOUISE'S VOICE   *Boy, you see what color I am.*

(Close-up: MALCOLM, staring at LUTHER.)

MALCOLM   *If God is black—?*

LUTHER   *That's right. You heard me. I knew you'd hear me. The white man is the devil. All white men are devils.*

OSTROVSKI'S VOICE   *Why don't you become a carpenter?*

(Close-up: MALCOLM, looking around him.
Pan: the white faces.)

136

LUTHER   *Tell me—have you ever known a good white man in all your life?*

MALCOLM   *I don't know.*

(Insert: MISS DUNNE.)

LUTHER   *Did you ever meet a black Christian wasn't down on his knees, begging the good Lord Jesus to give them in heaven what white people have here on earth?*

(Insert: the bloody rabbit, falling at the feet of LOUISE.
Insert [reversing the shot we have seen before]: EARL, his back to us, waving at LOUISE.)

LOUISE   *Earl!*

(Insert: EARL LITTLE on the trolley-car tracks.
Close-up: MALCOLM.
Pan: the white faces in the prison courtyard.
One of the white prisoners waves at a GUARD.)

LUTHER   *Have you ever met a white man who didn't hurt you?*

(MRS. SWERLIN, JUDGE MERRITT; MALCOLM, facing them, in the background.)

JUDGE MERRITT   *We're mighty proud of you, son.*

MRS. SWERLIN   *Oh, yes, Malcolm! And your mother would be so proud!*

(They turn away. MALCOLM does not move.)

(Exterior. Day. The prison courtyard.)

LUTHER   *We're a nation, lost in this wilderness for a long time.*

(Insert: LAURA and MALCOLM, running along the Cape Cod beach.
Insert: LAURA and DANIEL, in the bar.
Insert: ARCHIE, at the moment of the showdown.
Close-up: MALCOLM.)

LUTHER   *But now Allah has sent us a prophet who will help us clean up our lives—*

(Insert: SOPHIA, in an abandoned or orgiastic moment.
MALCOLM's face, dimly, intermittently seen in the surface of the shoes he is shining.
Two shot. LUTHER and MALCOLM.)

LUTHER   *You don't even know who you are. You don't even know, the white devil has hidden it from you —we're a race of people of ancient civilizations,*

rich, rich, in gold and in kings. You don't even
know your true family name, you wouldn't recognize your true language if you heard it. You have
been cut off by the devil, the devil white man, from
all true knowledge of your own kind. You have
been a victim of the evil of the devil white man ever
since he murdered and raped and stole you from
your native land in the seeds of your forefathers.—
He strangled us in the mind, man, in the mind—and
made us love him, while he was butchering us, made
us ashamed of ourselves and made us try to be like
him—to be like him—!

(Insert: MALCOLM flushing his head in the toilet
bowl.)

MALCOLM   That's true. That's true.

(Close-up: LUTHER and MALCOLM.)

LUTHER   But our God has always been a God of peace.
And life on this earth was a paradise, man, until the
white man used his tricks to betray us into bondage
and rise and rule the world. But his rule is ending
now. Our day is coming now. (Close-up: MAL-
COLM.) and now the white man will have to pay—
like we paid. And he's going to suffer and cry—like
we did. And there won't be nobody to hear him. Just
like there wasn't nobody to hear us.

MALCOLM *That'll be sweet. That'll be mighty sweet.*

LUTHER *You have any brothers?*

MALCOLM *Yes.*

LUTHER *I had a brother, older than me. We come up in Waycross, Georgia—way before your time.*

(Late afternoon, remembered time. A Georgia landscape.)

LUTHER'S VOICE *He had a fight with a white man about his wages. He said the man was cheating him, and God knows it was the truth.* (Exterior: empty porch of a Georgia company store. Interior: a scale swaying crazily inside the store.) *He knocked the white man down and then he come home to get a few things because he figured he'd better get out of town.* (Exterior: figures, indistinct, far away, begin gathering in the landscape.) *They caught him. That white man got his friends together—just about every white man for miles around—and they caught him. He hadn't got far.* (Exterior: shouts and yells and the people come closer.) *I was hiding in a ditch. I was real little then.*

(Exterior: from the child LUTHER's point of view: the feet of many men.

We hear male and female voices, jubilant, loud.

Beneath this, we are aware of a labored, agonized breathing.

From the child LUTHER's point of view: naked, black feet, being dragged.

We hear one lone, human, despairing scream.

Traveling close-up: the black man's sweating face.

Pan from the victim's point of view: the sun: very bright.

Close-up: hands gathering firewood.

Traveling shots: swift, blurred, distorted, of some of the faces of the people as the mob hurry their victim to the tree.

Close-up: the black man's neck as the rope goes around it. His eyes are closed.

Close-up: white hands on his naked black flesh as he is lifted by these hands, and the sun strikes on his body.

Blackout: as the child LUTHER puts his hands before his eyes.

Close-up: as the fire is lighted.

A great shout goes up.

Pan: with the smoke and the sparks upward, to stare straight into the sun.

Close-up: the fire rising.)

It was bright—bright. I couldn't see my brother. I couldn't hear him. I saw—

(Close-up: LUTHER's tormented, grown-up, possessed face.)

LUTHER   —*the sun darken*—

(Exterior: remembered time. The landscape darkens. The fire remains.)

LUTHER'S VOICE   *And then I knew my brother was gone. I saw the people*—

(Traveling shot: close, blurred, distorted, of the faces of the people: and some of these faces are full of terror and regret: some have the peace which follows an orgasm or a religious conversion.)

But they weren't people any more. They were—

(Close-up: LUTHER's grown-up, messianic eyes.
Traveling shot: a wolf leaps on his invisible prey, tearing it.
Close-up: the bloody jaws of the wolf.
Close-up: the black limbs against the bark of the tree, swinging slightly.
Close-up: wolves, rats, swine. All feeding. All bloody.
Pull back: all of them are feeding on the black, charred body which is now lying on the ground.

Pan: the sky. The sun, distant, veiled.)

Then I knew—

(Close-up: the people who have been animals turn into people again. Some of them are staring at the corpse, some have turned away.)

—that God had turned away from these people for-ever. They were trying to kill God because God was black and they knew it.

(Exterior. Dusk. Remembered time.
The people, quiet now, are beginning to leave. They leave the black corpse lying on the ground.
Traveling shot: toward this corpse, until the face of the dead man is in close-up.)

I looked into his face.

(Exterior. Remembered time: the sun.)

Then I knew that every time the devil called the white man attempts to kill God he brings his own destruction closer. He brings my vengeance nearer!

(Close-up: LUTHER.)

LUTHER   *Allah is not mocked forever.*

MALCOLM *All white men are devils—without any exception?*

LUTHER *Without any exception.*

MALCOLM *I knew a Jew once—who was very nice to me—*

LUTHER *Yeah. I know. He let you make five hundred dollars—while he was making ten thousand.*

MALCOLM *I guess that's true.—He's dead now.*

LUTHER *I knew somebody used to say: if you meet a good white man—shoot him before he turns bad.*

(A whistle blows. They walk out of the frame. The other prisoners follow.

They all reenter the prison.

Day. The prison lunchroom.

MALCOLM sits at the table, oblivious. He does not touch the food. From time to time, he sips a little water.

Two shot. LUTHER and PETE.)

PETE *What's the matter with Satan?*

LUTHER *He's deciding that it's better to serve in hell than rule in heaven.*

(PETE stares at him.
LUTHER laughs.)

LUTHER   *Don't worry about it. You'll never know.*

(Night. A weak light burning in the corridor outside MALCOLM's cell.

The GUARD passes, looking in at each cell.

Close-up: MALCOLM, on his bunk, waiting for the
GUARD to pass.

When the GUARD passes, he leaves his bunk. He is
carrying a book.

He lies flat on his belly before the cell door, reading
in the weak light which comes in from the corridor.)

MALCOLM (reading, under his breath)   *Saul—on the
road—to Damascus—*

(Day. MALCOLM's cell.

A gaunt MALCOLM sits there, staring.

Interior. Day. The prison lunchroom.

Two shot. LUTHER and PETE.)

PETE   *They tell me Satan is starving himself to death.
Or working on some act. He's a real hustler, that
one.*

LUTHER   *That's a whole lot more than I can say for you.*

145

(Interior. Day. MALCOLM's cell.

Shooting from below: from MALCOLM's point of view: the white DOCTOR enters MALCOLM's cell.)

DOCTOR *What's the matter with you, boy?*

MALCOLM *Nothing's the matter.*

DOCTOR *Why won't you eat?*

MALCOLM *Don't feel like eating.*

DOCTOR (making a perfunctory examination) *Whatever you're trying to pull, boy—you won't get away with it.*

(MALCOLM laughs. The DOCTOR stares.)

(Exterior. Day. The prison yard.
Two shot. MALCOLM and LUTHER.)

LUTHER *I wrote to the leader about you. He's going to be writing you.*

(Interior. Night. MALCOLM's cell.

He is lying flat on his belly, before the cell door, reading a letter in the light from the corridor.)

MALCOLM (reading) *"The key to a Muslim is submis-*

sion, the attunement of one toward Allah." (His hand gropes for the dictionary. But he continues to read.) *"The Messenger of Allah."*

(His hand finds a pencil.

Laboriously, he attempts to write. He is trying to write "Dear Sir." But he can scarcely form the letters, and we see that he does not know the spelling. The pencil breaks.

He hears the footsteps of the GUARD and crawls back into his bunk.

Day. MALCOLM's cell. MALCOLM, on his bunk, with the dictionary and pad and pencil, trying to write.

With at least every other word, he must stop and look in the dictionary.)

MALCOLM'S VOICE   *Dear Sir. The messenger of Allah. I cannot tell you how happy your teachings make me feel. You have made me understand why black men are in prison. I see how the devil is the white man. I wish I had understand this before. My life would have been different. Thank you. Yours sincerely. Malcolm Little. P.S. Thank you for the five dollars.*

(Jump shot. Day. MALCOLM, on his bunk, reading.)

MALCOLM'S VOICE   *Turn to Allah—pray to the East—*

(Day. The license-plate shop.
Two shot. LUTHER and MALCOLM.)

MALCOLM   *Luther—do you pray?*

LUTHER   *Yes.*

MALCOLM   *Why?*

LUTHER   *To learn submission to the will of Allah. We
all must learn to bow.*

MALCOLM   *The only times I ever went on my knees was
to pick a lock—something like that.*

LUTHER   *Well. This is the biggest lock you'll ever have
to pick.*

MALCOLM   *You said you were going to tell me how to
get out of prison.*

LUTHER   *Pick the lock.*

(Day. MALCOLM in his cell. He is sweating.
He looks around him, almost as though he were on
a crowded avenue.
He walks to the window of the cell.
Long shot, MALCOLM's point of view: the deserted
yard.

He walks to the door of the cell, peers out.

Long shot, MALCOLM's point of view: the empty corridor.

The prison is strangely silent.

MALCOLM walks to the center of the cell, folding his hands before him.

Slowly, awkwardly, he attempts to kneel.

Laughter breaks out somewhere nearby, and he rises hastily, sweating more than ever.

Night. MALCOLM's cell.

MALCOLM lies sleeping, tossing, dreaming.

The sound of a trolley-car.

Close-up: MALCOLM, asleep, sweating.

Over the image of MALCOLM:

Night. The streetcar tracks, the streetcar rushing toward the helpless body of EARL LITTLE.

MALCOLM sits up, nearly falling out of the bunk.

Over this image:

Night. The fire engulfing EARL LITTLE's house.

We move into the fire until the fire fills the screen.

Night. The cell.

Close-up: MALCOLM, staring.

He moves from the bunk into the middle of the floor.

He clasps his hands before him, and kneels down.

He looks up, but he is wordless.

He begins to weep. He bows his head.)

MALCOLM   *Forgive me. Forgive me. Forgive me.*

(Day. A prison corridor.

Traveling shot. A jubilant LUTHER, dressed in civilian clothes, walks the corridor.

He enters the license-plate shop.

The license-plate shop from LUTHER's point of view.

As he enters, a great cheer comes from the men.

Close-up: LUTHER, beaming.)

LUTHER *Well, just don't talk about me when I'm gone, that's all!*

(Medium shot. The men.)

PETE *Talk about you, hell! We can't wait to see the last of your black ass!*

FRANK *I'm sure going to miss your lectures about the Dahomey kings, and all.*

LUTHER *Hush up, Frank; every time I opened my mouth you as good as called me a liar.* (Long shot. MALCOLM, half seated, far in the back, watching all this, and smiling.) *Well, I ain't got long to stay here, men—you all remember the song. I got a train to catch. Let me have a minute with my man over yonder.* (He walks over to MALCOLM. Two shot. MALCOLM and LUTHER.) *Well. Here I go. You'll be following me soon.*

MALCOLM   *Yes, sir. I will.*

LUTHER   *Listen. I just want to tell you. You keep praying and working here. I'll be working and praying
outside. Me and the Leader will both be in constant
touch with you—so don't lose heart.*

MALCOLM   *I won't lose heart.*

LUTHER   *When you come out, you come straight to me.
We ain't got much, but what we got is yours, too.—
You like a son to me, Malcolm. Remember that.*

MALCOLM   *I'll remember. Thank you, Luther.*

LUTHER   *Don't thank me. Praise Allah. He did it.*

MALCOLM   *I do praise Allah. But I thank you, too.*

LUTHER   *Peace be unto you, Malcolm. As-Salaam-Alaikum.*

MALCOLM   *And unto you be peace. Wa-Alaikum-
Salaam.*

(LUTHER leaves. We hear his final good-byes to
the men.
We remain with MALCOLM.
We hear the door close behind LUTHER.)

MALCOLM (returning to work) *Allahu-Akbar. Allah is the greatest. Allahu-Akbar. Allahu-Akbar.*

(Sunday morning. The prison Bible class.
The class is taught by a young white man; to whom the prisoners—black and white—are not responding with great enthusiasm.)

THE TEACHER *The example that Jesus gives us, for example, in His Sermon on the Mount*—(Close-up: the traditional Jesus on a mount, before the traditional multitude.)—*is an example of love and humility. And it is a glorious example, given us by the very Son of God. When we truly understand Jesus, then we are able truly to love each other, even in prison, and to endure all things—even here —for Jesus is here with us—*

(Angle: MALCOLM puts up his hand.
Angle. THE TEACHER.)

THE TEACHER *Yes—?*

MALCOLM *That picture of Jesus there—is that a real picture?*

THE TEACHER *What do you mean?*

MALCOLM *I mean—is that the way he looked?*

THE TEACHER   *Well—it's not a* photograph. *It's a* repre-
sentation—*of Jesus.*

MALCOLM   *You mean, it's the way somebody imagined
Jesus looked?*

THE TEACHER   *Yes. You could say that.*

MALCOLM   *Well—my question is—*

(Close-up: MALCOLM.
Close-up: a few of the prisoners.)

MALCOLM   *—how could he imagine that Jesus was
white?*

(Close-up: PETE.
Close-up: THE TEACHER.)

THE TEACHER   *I'm not sure I understand you—*

(Close-up: FRANK.)

MALCOLM   *I mean, Jesus was a fisherman, for one thing.
Him, and all his disciples had to spend a lot of time
in the sun. So, he couldn't have looked like that—
like somebody who was never in the sun. And another thing—*

(Close-up: THE TEACHER: angry and uneasy.)

THE TEACHER   *It is a sacred picture. It's the way many believers have seen their Lord and Saviour.*

MALCOLM   *That means that Christianity is just a white man's religion—if that's the way they want us to see Jesus. What color was his disciples?—What color was Paul? He had to be black—because he was a Hebrew—and the original Hebrews—*

(*Swift* series of close-ups, black and white faces, listening intently, almost afraid.

Close-up: MALCOLM: intense, tense, and determined.)

MALCOLM   *—the original Hebrews were black—weren't they?*

(Close-up: THE TEACHER: trapped.
Pan: the black faces.
Close-up: THE TEACHER.)

THE TEACHER   *Yes.*

MALCOLM   *What color was Jesus?*

(Close-up: FRANK.)

MALCOLM   *What color was Jesus? He was Hebrew, too
    —wasn't he?*

    (Pan: the black and white faces, as they watch this
unheard-of contest.)

MALCOLM   *What color was Jesus?*

THE TEACHER   *Jesus—*

    (The faces waiting.)

THE TEACHER   *—Jesus was brown.*

    (Close-up: MALCOLM: perhaps a little smile.)

MALCOLM   *Thank you. Sir.*

    (Pan: the black faces, staring at MALCOLM.)

    (Day. The license-plate shop.
    Traveling shot: a GUARD, black or white.
    The traveling shot brings us to:
    Close-up: young PETE's face.
    PETE is listening to MALCOLM.
    Pull back: to discover that most of the MEN are
listening to MALCOLM.
    Traveling shot: The GUARD.)

MALCOLM'S VOICE   *—you ever before hear a white man tell you that Jesus wasn't white? Jesus brown!—*

(Close-up: MALCOLM, laughing.)

MALCOLM   *—a brown Jesus! and you heard the white man tell you that himself—*(He looks at the GUARD.)*—if that don't tell you what a liar the white man is—I don't know what else you need to hear.*

PETE   *Hey. Cool it, baby.*

MALCOLM (looking at the GUARD)   *Cool what? He knows he's a devil. He just don't want you to know it—*(To the GUARD) *Ain't that right?* (To the men) *And they tell us salvation is free!*

(Night. The prison corridor. We watch a GUARD walking.
Close-up: the light bulb in the corridor.
Close-up: MALCOLM's hand, writing.
We hear the GUARD's footsteps.
The hand tenses.
Close-up: MALCOLM's pad, on which he has written the word "rope."
Close-up: the light bulb in the corridor as the

GUARD passes before it, turning everything black—
briefly.

>Close-up: MALCOLM's face, in the light from the
light bulb.

>Close-up: MALCOLM's pad, on which he has written.

>Close-up: "Striving: to strive."

>Jump shot: interior. Another prison.

>MALCOLM's letter, being read by SHORTY.

>Close-up: SHORTY, reading.)

MALCOLM'S VOICE   *I don't know how to tell you that
I've found the truth. God is a man. God is a black
man. I had to come to prison to find this out. I do
not know the man yet, but I know the man who
knows the man—*

>(Close-up: MALCOLM's hand, laboriously writing.)

MALCOLM'S VOICE   *—this man has saved my soul. Listen, Shorty, don't drink no more and don't smoke
no more cigarettes and don't eat no more pork—*

>(Close-up: SHORTY, reading.)

MALCOLM'S VOICE   *—and I'll show you how to get out
of prison.*

>(SHORTY falls on his bunk, laughing.)

(Exterior. Bright midday.

MALCOLM, wearing prison glasses, walks out the prison doors.

And stands there for a moment, entirely alone.

As MALCOLM stands there, we examine him very carefully, head to toe: his prison shoes, his prison suit, the small package of his belongings under his arm.

Close-up: MALCOLM, squinting at the sun.

His glasses hurt him, and he takes them off.

He begins walking.

Traveling shot. MALCOLM's point of view: a young black messenger on a bicycle.

Close-up: MALCOLM, watching, squinting.

Pan: from the sun to the BOY.

Traveling shot: the BOY.

The sun through the trees, to:

Close-up: MALCOLM, squinting.

The BOY arrives at his destination: an enormous white hotel.

The BOY gets off his bike and enters the service entrance.

Close-up: the sign—SERVICE.

The BOY, disappearing into this darkness.

MALCOLM continues walking.

We see him reflected in the plate-glass window of a pawnshop.

Pan: the window, coming to rest on a wristwatch.

Then we hear water running, and discover this watch, and a new pair of glasses lying on a towel. Nearby is a brand-new suitcase. We are in a public bath.

We see MALCOLM bathing. His face is very peaceful.)

(Day. A printing press.

SIDNEY, who has been working this press, wipes his hands and comes, smiling, toward the camera.)

SIDNEY *Peace, brother—my daddy didn't tell me you'd be so tall!*

MALCOLM *Peace.*

SIDNEY *My dad's not home yet. He was having a meeting with some of the other ministers. But he won't be long. Sit down, make yourself at home. Can I get you something? A glass of milk? some fruit juice?*

MALCOLM *I'll have a glass of milk, if it's no trouble.*

(LORRAINE enters.)

SIDNEY *You meet my mother? Mama, this is the man Dad's been telling us so much about.*

LORRAINE *I knew that the moment I opened the door. How are you, son? It's a pleasure to see you.*

MALCOLM   *It's a pleasure for me, too, ma'am.*

SIDNEY   *Can I call you Malcolm?*

MALCOLM   *Sure, you can call me Malcolm. What's your name?*

SIDNEY   *My name is Sidney.*

LORRAINE   *He's Luther's right-hand man.*

SIDNEY   *That's what she says—but it's not true. She's my daddy's right-hand man—and she has been for as long as I can remember.—I'll get some milk.*

(He goes. LORRAINE and MALCOLM look at each other somewhat uneasily.)

LORRAINE   *So you met my husband in prison. You don't look old enough.*

MALCOLM   *No, ma'am. I wasn't very old.—But most people think I look older than I am.*

LORRAINE   *Most people don't see much.—So. You're going to be part of The Movement now.*

MALCOLM   *Yes, ma'am. I owe my life to The Movement. It opened my eyes—to the truth. The truth, espe-*

cially about the black man—and the devil called the white man.

LORRAINE   *Luther must be very proud of you.*

MALCOLM   *I hope so, ma'am. I hope so.*

LORRAINE   *Have you met the Leader?*

MALCOLM   *Not yet—but Luther says—the Leader wants to meet me. Can you imagine that?*

LORRAINE   *Yes. I can.*

MALCOLM   *And so Luther says we'll meet—sometime soon. I can't tell you—especially after Luther left —how much his teachings meant to me. And his letters. And sometimes he used to send me—a little money. It made me feel—excuse me ma'am, I don't know how to talk—like somebody—some black man—the greatest black man, I believe, in this country—cared about me. Cared about me! and all his black children like me. Oh—! you must have met him. What is he like?*

LORRAINE   *Well, he's not exactly a man like other men. He can't help that. Neither is my husband. You'll see. You'll see for yourself.*

MALCOLM *Have you been in The Movement long?*

LORRAINE *Since Luther went to prison. The Leader wrote him, too, and sent him money. And—opened my eyes—to many things.*

(SIDNEY returns, with a glass of milk.)

SIDNEY *I bet you thought I had to go and bring the cow home, didn't you? Well, I almost did—because there wasn't but just about half a glass left in the bottle. So I ran and got some.*

LORRAINE *Why didn't you bring him a piece of my chocolate cake?*

SIDNEY *Sorry, Mama.* (He starts out, turns.) *But women really are subordinate in this Muslim household, Malcolm.* (He goes.)

LORRAINE *Do you have any special thing you think you'd like to do in The Movement?*

MALCOLM *Whatever the Leader thinks I'm fit to do. I think I'd like to work on the paper—but I don't have no training—*

LORRAINE *You've got a lot of training—in being black. That's what you'll need.* (A door slams. LORRAINE rises.) *Well. Here he is.*

(LUTHER and SIDNEY enter, SIDNEY carrying a piece of cake.)

LUTHER   *So you're free at last.*

MALCOLM   *And free forever. Peace be unto you.*

LUTHER   *And unto you be peace—What do you think of this big-headed boy of mine? He tell you about the paper?*

SIDNEY   *He just got here, Daddy, let the man drink his milk.—It's just a little paper now. But we're going to make it a big one.*

LUTHER   *You know how it is in the white devil's press. He don't write nothing about black people to give us any pride in ourselves. Black people don't find out nothing they need to know in white papers.*

SIDNEY   *What it is, Malcolm—it's really a community newspaper—to let black people know what's going on in the black community—what they're doing themselves—*

LUTHER   *And what they* can *do. And what they've got to do.*

SIDNEY   *You should see what it means to the people.*

MALCOLM   *How do you get it distributed?*

(SIDNEY and LUTHER laugh.)

SIDNEY   *Distributed—!*

(Sunday morning. A holy-roller service in full swing.

Close-up: the church sign: THE NEW TESTAMENT CHURCH OF GOD IN CHRIST.

A dark, patient boy, carrying several copies of the paper, steps before this sign, holding up the paper.

A barroom. Music. Laughter.

Outside the bar, another dark, patient boy, with papers.

SIDNEY carrying papers into a pool hall, which is crowded.

MALCOLM and LUTHER enter a restaurant, both carrying papers.

Pan: the faces in the restaurant.)

LUTHER'S VOICE   *We got to make the people* aware *of what's happening to them—*

(Black mother and child in a Harlem window.)

LUTHER'S VOICE   *—and* why *it's happening—*

(Close-up: a young hustler in the pool hall, making his shot.

A young junkie, nodding on a stoop.)

LUTHER'S VOICE — *and make them know it's the white devil who's responsible for all this misery.*

SIDNEY *And then they—will change their situation themselves.*

MALCOLM *But how—are we going to make them aware?*

(Dusk. The streets of Harlem.)

MALCOLM'S VOICE OVER *Every time I walk these streets, I feel like somebody raised from the dead—* (Closeup: SIDNEY, walking with MALCOLM.)—*so many of us died here.* (We travel slowly up Seventh Avenue.) *I had a friend around here, a long time ago.* (We are climbing the dark stairs of a run-down rooming house.) *I just always wanted the cat to know that I would never, never, have lied to him.*

(A dark door comes closer and fills the screen and MALCOLM knocks.
MALCOLM and SIDNEY, their backs to us, in silhouette, SIDNEY behind MALCOLM, near the top of the stairs.
MALCOLM knocks again.
A voice from within responds, weakly.)

VOICE *Who is it?*

MALCOLM *It's me. Red.*

(A silence now falls, not so much broken as emphasized by a painful shuffling within the room.)

VOICE *Red—?*

MALCOLM *Country-boy.*

(The door is unlocked, and WEST INDIAN ARCHIE stands there, in a bathrobe. He is visibly old and ruined: but he is still ARCHIE.)

ARCHIE *Red. I'm mighty glad to see you. Come on in.*

(MALCOLM enters. When ARCHIE *sees* SIDNEY, fear crosses his face.)

MALCOLM *I just brought a friend—a young brother. This is Sidney. Sidney, this is my old friend, Archie.*

SIDNEY *How do you do, sir?*

ARCHIE *Not bad, son, considering. Make yourself welcome.—Red, where you drop from, boy? I didn't*

*think—excuse the way this place looks, but, you
know, I ain't been too well since Ada passed.*

MALCOLM   *Ada? What happened?*

ARCHIE   *Sit down. Sit down, son.—Ada. She had to
have one of them female operations, you know—it
come out of the Life—and she never, really, got no
better—and she passed—a year, come June. Yeah.
That's right.—How you been, Red? Heard you was
in trouble, awhile back—now, who told me that?
Couldn't of been Cadillac, he gone, too. No. Who
told me?*

MALCOLM   *How have you been?*

ARCHIE   *Oh, you know old West Indian Archie. Always
got something working. I'm figuring on going back
to the islands, couple of weeks. Like to see my
kinfolk. I got kin there I ain't never seen. Be ready
to go in a couple of weeks, I reckon. Just waiting
to close a deal I got in the works—I can't really
talk about it. You understand.*

MALCOLM   *Yes, sir. I do.*

ARCHIE   *Now, who told me you was in trouble? Somebody was after you, and you had to leave town.*

I wish I could remember who told me.—You all right now?

MALCOLM   *Oh, yes, sir. Yes, sir. I'm all right now.*

ARCHIE   *Well, that's good. I always thought the world of you, Red. Yes, sir. You was like a son to me.— You going to be in town for long?*

MALCOLM   *I—I can't say, sir. I—just wanted to see how you were.—We have to go now.*

ARCHIE   *Well, it was mighty nice of you to drop in, Red. —You, too, son. Come by and see me again.*

SIDNEY   *Yes, sir. I was glad to meet you, sir.*

ARCHIE   *Don't let Red steer you wrong. He's a good old boy, just a little stubborn, is all.—Red? You come and see me now, before I go back to the islands. I'm leaving soon, in a couple of weeks.*

MALCOLM   *Yes, sir. I'll remember that, sir.—Goodnight.*

ARCHIE   *Goodnight. You stay out of trouble. It hurt me to my heart to hear that you was in trouble.*

MALCOLM   *Goodnight.*

ARCHIE   *Goodnight, son.*

(As ARCHIE closes the door behind them, close-up of BETTY in her Muslim robes, in front of her class)

BETTY   *Well, that's the end of our lesson tonight, dear sisters—and perhaps I ought to include the dear brothers who have been eavesdropping outside the classroom.*

(The sisters turn, and laugh: and we see that three brothers have indeed been eavesdropping outside BETTY's evening class in the Temple: and the brothers are LUTHER, MALCOLM, and SIDNEY.
The class exits, graceful and shy with the brothers, and disappears. BETTY comes out last.)

LUTHER   *Now, Sister Betty, that final remark really was not nice at all. How long before you knew we was standing out here?*

BETTY   *How long before I knew? Brother Luther, you try to talk to a roomful of women about the Meaning of Marriage with three men standing outside the classroom.*

LUTHER   *But I'm married.*

BETTY   *They don't have to know that. And they know*

your son ain't married—how are you, Brother Sidney?

SIDNEY   *Getting anxious, Sister Betty, getting anxious!*

BETTY   *There, you see? and they taking bets about the other brother, this tall one, I can guarantee you.*

LUTHER   *This is Brother Malcolm. This is Sister Betty.*

(They touch hands, but do not speak. They all begin moving away from the classroom door.)

BETTY   *It's hard to teach a class with people eavesdropping—you know the only thing my class really wanted me to tell them?*

SIDNEY   *What?*

BETTY   *If Brother Malcolm was married.—Are you married, Brother Malcolm? I got to end the suspense, it's killing them.*

SIDNEY   *Tell them Brother Malcolm's not married, Sister Betty.*

BETTY   *You sound like you expect to be his best man.*

(Evening. The Harlem streets.

170

SIDNEY, with his papers.

Two black men are having a fist-fight—a fight not as serious as it is loud: and each man has his supporters in the crowd.

SIDNEY approaches the crowd. He recognizes a Muslim minister, and gets next to him.)

SIDNEY   *What's happening, brother?*

BROTHER HINTON   *Two fools. They don't know what they doing.*

(A patrol car speeds up, stops at the curb, and two POLICEMEN descend.)

POLICEMAN   *All right, that's enough! Break it up. Break it up!*

(The crowd immediately reacts: against the POLICE.)

VOICES   *Who the fuck you think you talking to? We don't need no crackers to help us settle our fights! You break it up, you white motherfuckers! Who you telling to go home? YOU go home!*

POLICE   *We said, Break it up! Break it up!*

(Close-up:)

SIDNEY (as we hear the effects of the night sticks. He begins moving backward.) *Get out the way, Brother Hinton.*

(SIDNEY speaks too late. BROTHER HINTON goes down beneath a night stick. SIDNEY jumps out of the way.

He stares about him for a moment, and then runs across the street, into a drugstore. As we watch him run, we also see that the use of the nightsticks is turning the people into a mob.

SIDNEY goes into a phone booth, dials a number.

The Temple: the phone rings.

MALCOLM picks it up.)

MALCOLM *You stay where you are, Brother Sidney.— No. Wait a minute. You call every minister you can get your hands on, and have them meet me in front of the police station.—Yes. Right away.*

(MALCOLM hangs up, and begins dialing.

We watch the Muslim ministers gathering in front of the police station. They are very disciplined, and line up in military formation.

But other people join them, coming out of houses, off of stoops, and out of bars.

From within the police station, we see the uneasy reaction to this silent, gathering, not-yet mob.)

A MUSLIM MINISTER (addressing the people) *Be quiet,*

brothers. *Don't give the white devil no excuse to kill. He so sick, killing is the only thing he know how to do. They tried to kill one of our brothers tonight, and that's why we here. This time, we ain't going to let them get away with it. But, just be quiet. We'll let you know what's happening.*

(MALCOLM arrives, with other ministers, and SIDNEY, and enters the police station.)

MALCOLM   *I am Minister Malcolm X, of Temple Number Seven, and you have one of our fellow ministers here, and we demand to see him.*

CAPTAIN   *Never heard of your temple, mister, and don't know nothing about your brother. I'd say you in the wrong place.*

MALCOLM   *You have beaten and imprisoned a certain Minister Hinton, you have him on the premises, we demand to see him, and we have eyewitness proof of the beating.*

CAPTAIN   *Eyewitness, huh?*

MALCOLM   *One, standing next to me—others, outside.* (A pause) *Shall I bring them in?*

CAPTAIN (to SIDNEY)   *You an eyewitness? You don't look old enough.*

173

SIDNEY *That's because you don't know how soon I started watching you.*

CAPTAIN *You standing there telling me you saw one of my men beat up somebody, for no reason, and you're prepared to swear to it?*

SIDNEY *I saw one of your filthy cops smash a man's skull in for no reason at all, and I swear to it!*

MALCOLM *Shall I bring in the other witnesses?*

CAPTAIN *You know, Mac, this is a police station—*

MALCOLM *That's why we're here.*

SIDNEY (under his breath) *Mac.*

CAPTAIN (looks at MALCOLM) *What's the name?*

MALCOLM *Hinton.*

CAPTAIN *Let me see the blotter.*

(The blotter is produced.
The CAPTAIN studies it.)

CAPTAIN *Oh, yeah, we got a Hinton, all right. We got*

him for resisting arrest. I'm afraid you can't see
him tonight.

MALCOLM *When* can *we see him?*

CAPTAIN *Can't say. Come back in the morning, that's
your best bet.*

MALCOLM *That's* your *best bet. Not* a *man of us will
move, before we see the brother.*

(From the CAPTAIN's point of view, we see the silent
crowd in the street: and it is their silence which makes
them frightening.)

CAPTAIN *You want that whole crowd to see him?*

MALCOLM *Do* you?—*We* will *see him, and report to the
people outside. The people are waiting for our report. That's why they are here. We called them
here. And they will not leave before they hear our
report.*

CAPTAIN (after a moment: turns) *Hey, Jerry!*

(The cell. The badly beaten, unconscious brother.
MALCOLM, SIDNEY, the CAPTAIN.)

MALCOLM *Come back in the morning? Is that what you*

said? Were you planning to have him buried by
morning? Don't you know this man needs a doctor?
Or don't you know he's a man?

CAPTAIN   Now, listen, Mac—

MALCOLM   My name ain't Mac. You listen. You send
for an ambulance right now and get this man to a
hospital. Right now.

CAPTAIN   Since when do you give the orders around
here?

MALCOLM   If you spend much more time asking funny
questions, you going to find yourself answering
some.—You want that pension, don't you? Well,
you better get on that phone.—You dog.

CAPTAIN   What did you call me?

MALCOLM   I take it back. A dog wouldn't do this.

(As the ambulance starts up the avenue, toward the
hospital, the ministers, led by MALCOLM, fall into line
behind it. People join them, mostly in silence, and, by
the time they line up before Harlem Hospital, they are a
considerable multitude.

Here, too, they stand in silence: and now the authorities realize that they are before a situation which will be by no means easy to control.

MALCOLM, a few ministers, and SIDNEY enter the hospital.

A POLICE CHIEF approaches MALCOLM.)

POLICE CHIEF *Look here, I just want to say how sorry we are about this mistake. It shouldn't have happened. Some crazy rookie just lost his head. It's too bad, and we do everything we can to prevent it—but —it happens, sometimes.*

SIDNEY *You must have a lot of rookies on the force.*

MALCOLM *The only mistake you made was letting a brother get to a phone booth.*

POLICE CHIEF *I can appreciate how you feel, one hundred per cent. But what's done is done. We don't want any more trouble tonight. Don't you think the people outside ought to go home?*

MALCOLM *These are the brother's fellow ministers. They were called here by me, and I can't send them away. And why should I? They're perfectly disciplined, standing there quietly and harming no one.*

POLICE CHIEF *But the others, the ones behind them— they're not disciplined.*

MALCOLM   *Oh, well, then, send the others home. The
    others are your problem.*

(The POLICE CHIEF stares at MALCOLM, stares out at
the crowd.)

POLICE CHIEF   *I just don't want to see any more blood-
    shed. Bloodshed never solved anything.*

MALCOLM   *It did, for you, just as long as the blood was
    ours.* (Addressing the crowd) *Brothers, sisters, I
    want to thank you for your patience, for that pa-
    tience has helped us to save a life. We have seen
    the brother, and we have spoken to the doctors. The
    brother is much better than he was before—before
    your presence forced the white devils to give him
    decent care. Everything that can be done is being
    done, and we feel satisfied that we can end our vigil
    tonight and go home and get some rest for the many
    vigils that are coming. There will be many. I want
    every man, woman, and child here tonight to re-
    member that if you hadn't been here, our brother
    might be dead. But, as long as we keep on doing
    like we did tonight, our brothers and sisters will
    live.*

(The crowd cheers MALCOLM, and slowly begins to
disperse.)

VOICE OF RADIO COMMENTATOR OVER —*it is true that the young Malcolm X handled a potentially explosive situation with considerable skill. But it can perhaps be argued that no one man should have such power.*

(Close-up: MALCOLM in a gale of flash-bulbs:)

MALCOLM *I don't know if I could start a riot. I don't know if I'd care to stop one.*

(Night. MALCOLM, walking slowly, in the vicinity of 110th Street and Lenox Avenue, on his weary way home.
A rather battered-looking black woman comes out of a bar near the subway, cursing.)

WOMAN *Ain't that some shit! You black motherfuckers can all kiss my ass.* Kiss my big black ass. *Since when you seen me strung out? Shit. You all be crying another tune tomorrow. I be straight tomorrow, and don't want to see none of you all come sucking around me. Shit!*

(She is weeping. She starts down the subway steps, stops under the light, digging in her purse.
A shadow—MALCOLM's—falls on her, and, abruptly, she looks up.
We see that it is LAURA—a ravaged, ruined, ancient

LAURA, with yet something in her of the girl that we once knew.

We watch her slow recognition of MALCOLM: she seems to crawl miles through a tunnel before a light breaks in her face.)

LAURA   *It's not you. It's not: you.—Malcolm?*

MALCOLM   *Laura. You a sight for sore eyes.* (He regrets this the moment he says it. Quickly:) *You going my way this time? The last time I saw you, you was headed in the opposite direction.*

LAURA   *I don't know. How've you been?* (Closes her purse.) *I was going uptown.*

MALCOLM   *I was, too. You want to have a cup of coffee, before we get on that noisy subway?*

LAURA   *Sure. Only, maybe, I'd rather have a drink.* (She comes back up the steps, looks toward the bar she has just left.) *But not in there. Nothing but jive mothers in there, and false friends.* (They begin walking.) *Funny running into you—in the subway!* (She laughs.)

(A very sleazy, rough bar, at least as rough as it is "gay." So loud that the roar of sound protects one's privacy.

LAURA and MALCOLM, on bar stools, far in the back.
MALCOLM is sipping a Coke.
LAURA is not drunk, but she is not sober.)

LAURA   *Daniel didn't force me to turn on. I know that's what people said, but it's not what happened. In fact, he didn't want me to know anything about it. But I had to find out—what it was—what it was— for him. Because I loved him, and that white lady was taking him away from me, and, this time, I swore I was going to have the courage to follow him. And I followed him.—Can I have another drink? It's funny to see you drinking Coca-Cola. Like a preacher.*

MALCOLM   *Sure, Laura.—I am—a minister.*

LAURA   *A minister?*

MALCOLM   *A Muslim minister.*

LAURA   *A what?* (To the [invisible] BARTENDER) *Do it again, Jake.*

MALCOLM   *I've found out many things, Laura. Many beautiful things. Maybe we could talk one day. Wouldn't you like to? Listen. The Temple isn't far from here, I can give you the address and the phone number and I can give you my address—*

181

(She has been watching him. She picks up her new drink.)

LAURA   *So you can convert me?*

MALCOLM   *No. We can just talk. I can tell you what's happened to me and how I found out—how I found Allah—how He found me, and how black people don't have to suffer like we suffer, we can live!*

LAURA   *You sound like my grandmother.*

MALCOLM   *I know. I guess it's got to sound funny, coming from me. But I know what I'm talking about, Laura, I really do. And my life has changed. People change, Laura.*

LAURA   *I know they do.*

MALCOLM   *Let me write down the address, anyway—*

LAURA   *No.*

MALCOLM   *Just in case—*

LAURA   *In case of what? In case I find I can't make these streets no more? No. Don't bother with me, Malcolm. It's too late. You could have done something for me, once—*

MALCOLM *When was that, what was that? Maybe I can again.*

LAURA *You could have married me. You certainly can't marry me now.—Can you?* (Laughs.) *Life's a bitch. You went away and here came Daniel and by the time that was over and Daniel was gone, I had turned so many tricks, for Daniel and for me, I couldn't stand another man's hands on me—not for love. The only way you could marry me now would be for you to have a boy friend on the side. I don't go that way no more, except for bread.—You're funny. You're shocked. Why are ministers always shocked? You're supposed to know more about life than other people, not less.*

MALCOLM *Laura—all I know is—God is great. I know there's love and hope. If you really want it—there's hope. We can change.*

LAURA *Malcolm, when a dress is torn, you can sew it up, make it do a little while longer. But when a dress is in rags—you just have to throw it away. You can't mend what's past mending. I know that.— Maybe, one of these awful days—you're going to have to find that out.*

MALCOLM (after a moment) *I'll write down the address, anyway.*

(He scribbles on a piece of paper, and hands it to her. She looks at it thoughtfully, puts it in her purse. She lights a cigarette.)

LAURA *What I really need, Malcolm, is subway fare.*

MALCOLM *I'll give you what I have.—There. That help?*

LAURA *Thanks. That way, my old man won't beat my ass. I might even have considered coming up to your Temple—but I know she'd never go for it.*

MALCOLM *Well, you've got the address.—I have to go, now. Goodnight, Laura.*

LAURA *Goodnight, Malcolm. You're still the very nicest boy I ever met.*

(He goes. She stays where she is, watching him.)

(MALCOLM and BETTY are surrounded by Muslim brothers and sisters. Much hand-shaking and embracing. LUTHER, LORRAINE, and SIDNEY are prominent. MALCOLM is almost ridiculously severe: he is trying to hide his happiness. This has the effect of making him seem even younger than he is.)

MALCOLM   *Now, I'm not going to be picking you up and carrying you over no doorsteps, now, and all like that—*

BETTY   *If I wanted to be picked up and carried over doorsteps, Brother Malcolm, I would certainly never have married you.*

MALCOLM   *All that Hollywood stuff—just turns foolish women's heads—*

SIDNEY   *He laying down the law to you already, Sister Betty? and you all ain't even got home yet!*

BETTY   *Oh, he's going to turn me into a real good Muslim wife, Brother Sidney.*

LORRAINE   *Well, you just make sure that he's a good Muslim husband, too, Sister Betty.* (Embraces her.) *You look beautiful today. I know you must be happy. Stay beautiful. Be happy.* (To MALCOLM)

I know you'll make her a wonderful husband, Mal-
colm.

MALCOLM *Yes, ma'am. I'm going to try.*

LORRAINE *You're going to do better than try.*

LUTHER *It was written. It was written. You just needed*
one thing to be complete. And now you're ready.
All praise is due to Allah. (Kisses BETTY.) *Allah*
has given you a husband who will do great things.

BETTY *I know that, Brother Luther.* (Kisses him.)
Thank you.

A MUSLIM SISTER *So, you got him!—Congratulations,*
Brother Malcolm.

MALCOLM *Thank you, Sister.—What does she mean—*
you got me?

BETTY *You know how women are, Malcolm. They just*
say the first thing that pops into their heads.

MALCOLM *You got me—!*

BETTY *Well, whichever way it was—whoever got who*
—I'm glad the suspense is over.

MALCOLM   *The suspense——?*

BETTY   *Why yes. It was almost killing those poor sisters. When I would wait around in the cafeteria for
you, some sister would always say, I got room right
here, Sister Betty. And I'd say, No, thank you, Sister, I'll wait. So——they knew all along.*

MALCOLM   *They knew——?*

BETTY   *They knew something——you know how women
are.*

MALCOLM   *I don't know if I know as much as I thought
I knew.*

A MUSLIM SISTER   *Congratulations, Brother Malcolm!
Congratulations, Sister Betty. How does it feel to be
first lady?*

BETTY   *First lady?*

MUSLIM SISTER   *That's what you are now.*

MALCOLM   *Sister, the Honorable Messenger is the only
first, and his wife is the only first lady. All of the
rest of us are just humble ministers for the Messenger of Allah.*

(Night. The airport.
MALCOLM and BETTY, alone.)

MALCOLM *Well, we just got married and already we
got to separate.*

BETTY *Just for a couple of days. It all happened so
suddenly. I didn't have time to get somebody to re-
place me.*

MALCOLM *It might not be easy, you know, Betty, being
married to a man like me. We might be separated
a lot. Awakening this brainwashed black man and
telling this arrogant, devilish white man the truth
about himself is a full-time job.*

BETTY *I've understood all that all along, dear heart.
I want you to work for The Movement. I belong to
The Movement, too. And I have a job to do, now.
My job is to be your wife. And I will do—the very
best job I can.*

MALCOLM *Allah be praised for you, Betty.*

BETTY *Allah be praised for you.*

(Her flight is announced. They walk to the gate.)

MALCOLM *I guess you're the only woman, Betty, I ever
dreamed of loving.*

(They look at each other.)

BETTY   *As-Salaam-Alaikum.*

MALCOLM   *Wa-ALAIKUM-Salaam.*

(They embrace. She goes.)

(We are before a television screen, and a NEGRO LEADER is speaking.)

NEGRO LEADER   *Make no mistake: these so-called Black Muslims we've been hearing so much about are just a handful of embittered racial fanatics, and they do not represent the Negro masses. It is an irresponsible hate cult—*

(Cut to: a WHITE NEWSCASTER.)

WHITE NEWSCASTER   *—a deplorable reverse-racism, a most unfortunate development just when the racial picture is beginning to improve—*

(Cut to: an exceedingly angry MALCOLM, in Close-up. Day.)

A VOICE   *Mr. Malcolm X, why do you teach black supremacy and hate?*

MALCOLM   *The white man so guilty of white supremacy and hate can't hide his guilt by trying to accuse the Honorable Messenger of teaching black supremacy and hate! All the Honorable Messenger is doing is trying to uplift the black man's mentality and the black man's social and economic condition in this country.*

(Cut to: a black boy, pushing a truck in the garment center.
The hosing-down of the children in Birmingham.)

MALCOLM'S VOICE OVER   *For the white man to ask the black man if he hates him is just like the rapist asking the raped or the wolf asking the sheep, "Do you hate me?"*

(Cut to: close-up of a southern sheriff.)

The white man is in no moral position to accuse anyone else of hate!

(Cut to: police dogs being used on children.
Police on horseback using cattle prods on men, women, and children.)

Why, when all my ancestors are snake-bitten and I'm snake-bitten and I warn my children to avoid

snakes, what does that snake *sound like accusing* me
of hate-teaching?

(Cut to: an incredibly overcrowded Harlem school.

Black adolescents playing cards and cursing and
smoking reefers on the stoop.

White men playing golf.)

*Christianity is the white man's religion. Every coun-
try the white man has conquered with his guns, he
has always paved the way and salved his conscience
by carrying the Bible and interpreting it to call the
people "heathens" and "pagans"—*

(Cut to: a weary black woman, climbing dark tenement stairs.

BETTY, teaching a Muslim class, the Muslim flag
prominent in the background.

The Flower of Islam: a karate class.

Black men, silently, in a barber shop, reading The
Movement's newspaper.)

*We, the followers of the Honorable Messenger of
Allah are today in the ghettoes as once the sect of
Christianity's followers were like termites in the
catacombs and the grottoes—and they were preparing the grave of the mighty Roman empire!*

(Day. Close-up: a weary young JUNKIE, leaning against a lamppost.

He sees someone approaching, and his face comes to life.

We see MALCOLM, walking fast, on the other side of the street.

The JUNKIE waves and smiles.)

JUNKIE   *Brother Malcolm! My man!*

(MALCOLM waves and smiles.)

(Day. SIDNEY, in the newspaper office. He is on the phone, listening, and what he is hearing displeases him and baffles him.

He is holding a photograph of MALCOLM. As he listens, from time to time trying to speak, he picks up various typed copies of stories on MALCOLM, and various other photographs:

MALCOLM, addressing eight thousand students in California.

MALCOLM, addressing a Harlem rally.

Various clippings concerning MALCOLM, in the white press.)

SIDNEY   *Dad, I don't want to sound insubordinate, or anything, but I don't see that. He's never—but that's all he's been doing—working for The Movement! Look—you said yourself you never saw anybody*

work so hard, with such devotion—Dad—? And the
Honorable Messenger said so, too, he said it in pub-
lic!—I know that, but you're my father, I got a right
to tell you what I think. All right. All right. But I
just hope you and the Honorable Messenger know
what you're doing, that's all, because I sure don't
—What? I'm sorry. Yeah. Sure. Good-bye.

(He hangs up, deeply distressed, allows the photograph of MALCOLM to fall from his hands into the waste-
basket, sits there.)

(Evening. BETTY, at home, the newspaper in her
lap.

She hears MALCOLM at the front door and throws
down the paper, rising as MALCOLM enters. He is very
tired.)

BETTY   *As-Salaam-Alaikum.*

MALCOLM   *Wa-Alaikum-Salaam.—The children asleep?*

BETTY   *Yes. It wasn't easy. They were determined to*
wait up for you. They complain that they never see
you.

MALCOLM   *They're right. I couldn't get away from this*
white devil of a reporter and then I had to visit a

couple of other places—tomorrow, I've got to be
in Boston for a television show, and a lecture—

BETTY   *Your children will not be pleased.*

MALCOLM   *I know.—What do you tell them?*

BETTY   *I tell them you are present when you are away.*

MALCOLM   *They don't understand that.*

BETTY   *Oh, yes, they do. They see you on television.—*
What time is your plane?

MALCOLM   *Ten o'clock. In the morning.*

BETTY   *I'll heat up supper so you can get a good night's*
sleep. How long will you be gone?

MALCOLM   *Just overnight. I'm speaking at the Har-*
vard Law School Forum.

(BETTY goes into the kitchen. MALCOLM sits down
wearily, takes off his shoes, leans back. He picks up the
paper, looks at it, puts it down, sits with his head back,
thinking.

BETTY reenters.)

BETTY   *Everything will be ready in a few minutes. Did*
you talk to Luther today?

MALCOLM   *No. I was too busy. And he stays busy.*

(BETTY starts to say something, stops. Then:)

BETTY   *Isn't it funny the paper didn't carry a word about your California rally?*

MALCOLM   *Might have been too late for the deadline, I guess.*

BETTY   *All the other papers carried it. You get more coverage in the white devil's press than you do in your own.*

MALCOLM   *Well, I'm just one minister, Betty. They probably figure that I don't need as much coverage as—*

BETTY   *Black people need to know what you're doing. That's what the paper was started for.*

MALCOLM   *To let black people know what I'm doing?*

BETTY   *You know that isn't what I mean. I mean, it's very important for black people to know the work that's being done in The Movement—so they will feel it's their Movement. And you do a lot of work. That's all.*

MALCOLM   *I'm not the most important thing in The Movement, Betty.*

(Close-up: BETTY: reluctantly deciding not to contradict him.)

BETTY   *Well, I just think it's a tactical error—not to cover your activities at least as thoroughly as the white devil's press does—*

MALCOLM   *Black people haven't got to be told what I'm doing. They* know *what I'm doing, they see me every day. It's* white *people who have to be told.*

BETTY   *I can't help feeling—I'm sorry—that there's something wrong.*

MALCOLM   *Well, you know that me and Luther—and the Honorable Messenger—have had little disagreements about policy. I'd like The Movement to be a little more* active—*to get out there in the streets more, maybe, and be—more* political—*but that doesn't mean there's anything wrong.*

BETTY   *A whole lot of people are very jealous of you, Malcolm, you know that.*

MALCOLM   *Oh—don't worry about that. I guess that always happens. The Honorable Messenger himself warned me that that would happen. Luther, and the Honorable Messenger, they know what I'm doing, they know why. They know I'm not trying to get anything for myself.*

BETTY *Malcolm—don't you think it's time, maybe, that you did think a little bit about that?*

MALCOLM *About what?*

BETTY *About your family—about us—*

MALCOLM *What are you getting at?*

BETTY *Malcolm, we have three children, and we're going to have a fourth—and we don't have a penny put aside—not even for doctors' bills and things like that.*

MALCOLM *We have access to money. The Honorable Messenger will always authorize as much money as I need.*

BETTY *Well—that isn't exactly what I mean—*

MALCOLM *What do you mean?*

(BETTY is silent.)

MALCOLM   *Betty, you knew when you married me that I was a minister. And you knew what that meant. It meant that as long as breath was in me, I would devote every single breath to Allah and the Honorable Messenger. Why, I would have no life if it hadn't been for the Honorable Messenger! You knew all that. So what are you trying to say to me now?*

BETTY   *I'm just saying that you ought to be thinking about your family. We have children now!—I bet you Luther thinks about his family!*

MALCOLM   *What do you mean?*

BETTY   *Just what I said.*

MALCOLM   *Luther is just as devoted a servant of Allah as I am! He brought me the light when I was in prison. How can you think such things about him?*

BETTY   *I don't think anything about him, except that he's a family man and he acts like he's a family man.*

MALCOLM   *Betty, I'm taking care of my family. We have the house. We have the car.*

BETTY   *We do not have the house. This house belongs to*

The Movement. We don't have anything—that's all I'm saying—

MALCOLM   *Look, I have seen too many organizations destroyed by their leaders because the leaders tried to benefit personally. And you know who goaded them to do it? Their wives.*

BETTY   *Malcolm, if you'd only listen—*

MALCOLM   *I am listening. You're asking me to use my ministry to benefit personally. And I'm telling you that I won't do it.*

BETTY   *Malcolm, what's going to happen to us if anything happens to you?*

MALCOLM   *Now, that's a foolish question. You're a Muslim. You know The Movement. You know the Honorable Messenger. You know Luther. Do you think they're going to let you starve? or the family of any other minister? What's the matter with you?*

BETTY   *What's the matter with you? I know Luther brought you the light in prison. That was a long time ago. Have you looked at Luther lately?*

MALCOLM   *What's the matter with Luther—lately?*

BETTY *Nothing.*

MALCOLM *I wish I knew what was going on in your mind.*

BETTY *I'm afraid. That's what's going on in my mind.*

MALCOLM *But you've nothing to be afraid of. If anything happens to me, The Movement will take care of you and the girls for the rest of your lives. I know that. That's a promise. You know that, too.*

BETTY *All right. Come on and eat.*

MALCOLM *Don't you believe me?*

BETTY *Yes. I believe you. I believe you.—Go. Wash up. I'll put supper on the table.*

(MALCOLM goes. BETTY stands still, watching him.)

(Day. BETTY, in the Harlem streets, walking very fast.

We follow her into the newspaper office, which is now far more like a real office than it has been before. She walks through the crowded and busy anteroom and knocks on SIDNEY's door.)

SIDNEY *Come on in.* (BETTY enters the office. SIDNEY,

surprised and pleased, rises.) *Sister Betty. What a nice surprise. What brings you this way?*

BETTY   *I just thought I'd come and see how my brother was doing.*

SIDNEY   *Well, that's mighty nice of you. Sit down.*

(BETTY does so, looks around the cluttered office.)

BETTY   *So—they keeping you pretty busy—?*

SIDNEY   *Yes, Sister Betty, they keeping me pretty busy. But the paper's circulation keeps growing—so you know I'm not complaining.*

BETTY   *You and Malcolm should be awfully proud. You two practically created this paper.*

SIDNEY   *Yeah—me and Malcolm—*

BETTY   *Sidney, I want to ask you a question, as long as I'm here. May I?*

SIDNEY   *Of course.*

BETTY   *I've been hearing things—about Malcolm— little things, here and there—I don't know how seriously to take them—*

SIDNEY   *What kind of things have you been hearing?*

BETTY   *Some people seem to feel that Malcolm's getting too big for his britches—that all the publicity he's been getting has gone to his head.—You must have heard it, too, Sidney.*

SIDNEY   *Well, there'll always be jealous people around, Sister Betty. I wouldn't let that kind of talk bother me.*

BETTY   *Have you heard it?*

SIDNEY   *Well, naturally, I would have to hear some of that kind of talk—but I've never let it worry me. It's just idle talk. People have to talk about somebody —nobody ever talks about me! I guess they don't think I'm interesting enough.*

BETTY   *They say that Malcolm's only interested in him-self—that he's only using The Movement—*

SIDNEY   *Well, that's just nonsense.*

BETTY   *Some people even say that he's beginning to be a danger to The Movement—that he should be sus-pended—or—even—expelled.*

SIDNEY   *You don't believe that!*

BETTY   *I don't know what I believe. But I know that there hasn't been a word about Malcolm in this paper for weeks. I want to know why. I know it can't be because of you. So there has to be some other reason.*

SIDNEY   *Some people have felt that Malcolm was maybe getting a disproportionate share of press coverage. So—I've been soft-pedaling for a while.*

BETTY   *Was it your idea?*

SIDNEY   *Not—not exactly.*

BETTY   *It's a blackout, then. A temporary blackout.*

SIDNEY   *I guess you could call it that.*

BETTY   *What else is there to call it? How long will it last?*

SIDNEY   *Not long.*

BETTY   *How do you know?*

SIDNEY   *Well, it can't last long, that's all. People be coming to their senses soon.*

BETTY   *Brother Sidney: do you really believe that?*

SIDNEY   *It stands to reason, Betty. The Movement needs Malcolm. People know that. Malcolm practically made The Movement what it is today. People can't forget that.*

BETTY   *Don't be too quick to say what people can't forget.—Were you ordered to keep Malcolm's name out of the paper?*

SIDNEY   *I wouldn't say I was ordered—*

BETTY   *You were told. Were you told why?*

SIDNEY   *I told you. Some people think Malcolm's been getting too much publicity.*

BETTY   *That's what you were told. But we both know that's not the reason.*

SIDNEY   *Then—I don't know the reason. But I'd try not to worry too much about it—if I were you.*

BETTY   *You're worried about it. And you know more about it than I do.*

SIDNEY   *It'll pass. It'll blow over. People get jealous, that's all.*

BETTY   *Malcolm's given his life to The Movement, and*

to the Honorable Messenger. He trusts your father as though it were his father.

SIDNEY   *I know.*

BETTY   *Does your father trust Malcolm?*

SIDNEY   *He doesn't have any reason not to. You know that.*

BETTY   *We know that. But you haven't answered my question.*

SIDNEY   *Sister Betty, I can't answer it. You know I'd answer if I could.*

BETTY   *I know that, dear heart.*

SIDNEY   *Do you and Malcolm have any money saved?*

BETTY (after a moment)   *No.*

SIDNEY   *With three children—*

BETTY   *It's soon going to be four.*

SIDNEY   *Oh, Sister Betty—I wish—!*

BETTY   *How do most people feel—about what's being done to Malcolm?*

SIDNEY   *Oh, we don't like it. We think it's wrong. (A pause.* BETTY *looks at him.) I don't understand it. I —don't—think I understand it.*

BETTY   *Dear heart. Malcolm and I—we trust you, you know.*

SIDNEY   *You can. You can trust me.*

BETTY   *I know. That's why I came to see you.*

SIDNEY   *It'll pass. You'll see. It'll be all right.*

BETTY   *I just wanted to know what's happening. It's terrible to be in the dark, wondering and worrying. I've thought I was going almost crazy. And Malcolm, he's so trusting, and so wrapped up in his work, and that makes it hard.—I don't see any reason to tell him that we talked. I'll tell him I was here, but that's all.—And now I'll let you get back to work. Why don't you come and have dinner with us tonight? Malcolm would love to see you.*

SIDNEY   *I'll try.*

BETTY   *Don't try. Be there.—And don't look so troubled.*

SIDNEY   *I don't—understand it.*

BETTY *I think you do. You wish you didn't. So do I.—*
     I'll make some corn bread. And we'll wait for you.

SIDNEY *All right.*

BETTY *Peace.*

SIDNEY *Peace.*

(After a moment, BETTY goes.

SIDNEY walks to the window, and stands there.

We look, with him, into the sky; and at this moment, we hear a shot.

Then we hear a cacophony of voices, in all the languages of the earth, rising to crescendo, with one word repeated over and over: Dallas. Dallas. Dallas.

We see the flags of nations, and the American flag, being lowered to half-mast.

A voice informs us: "—in the city of Dallas, Texas, today, President John Fitzgerald Kennedy—!"

A teletype machine clatters out a message:

All Muslim ministers are directed to maintain silence concerning the assassination of President Kennedy. If pressed, all Muslim ministers are directed to say, No comment.)

(Evening. The Manhattan Center, crowded.

MALCOLM is answering questions from the crowd.)

A WHITE MAN *What do you think about President Kennedy's assassination? What is your opinion?*

MALCOLM *Sir, it seems to me a clear case of chickens coming home to roost. Speaking as an old farm boy, I was never sorry when chickens came home to roost, I was glad. It is the American climate of hate which has struck down the President—that same climate of hate which has struck down so many black men for so long. But nobody cared as long as it was only black people. And now the hate that America has allowed to spread unchecked menaces every white man, woman, and child in America. Maybe it's a terrible kind of justice.*

(Close-up: LUTHER.)

LUTHER *What possessed you to say such a thing? when the Honorable Messenger had specifically instructed all of his ministers to say nothing?*

(We are in LUTHER's living room. MALCOLM and LUTHER are alone.)

MALCOLM *Luther, I said what I honestly felt. All right, maybe I didn't think. It was the question-and-answer period. As far as I was concerned, I wasn't talking to the press—but—all right—I made a mistake—*

LUTHER *A statement like that can make it very hard on all Muslims—do you realize that?*

MALCOLM *No. I don't really see that. Maybe you ought to spell it out to me a little.*

LUTHER *Malcolm, the whole country loved this man. The whole country is in mourning.*

MALCOLM *Is it?*

LUTHER *Don't split hairs with me. You know what I mean.*

MALCOLM *It just seems to me you're talking to me as though we didn't know each other—*

LUTHER *We are both servants of the same God, Malcolm, and his name is Allah. Our ministry comes before anything else. It comes before you. It comes before me. If I sound as though I don't know you— perhaps that's why.*

MALCOLM *I've said much more dangerous things than I said about the assassination, and I was never reprimanded before. And I haven't said anything that hundreds of other people aren't saying.*

LUTHER *Whatever others may have said is not our con-*

cern. And it's not even so much a matter of what you *said. You were directed to say nothing and you disobeyed. How can you expect to discipline others if you are not disciplined yourself?* (MALCOLM is silent.) *The Leader—the Honorable Messenger— has instructed me to inform you that you have been silenced for ninety days. That will give us time to dissociate all Muslims from your blunder.*

MALCOLM   *I will go to the Honorable Messenger myself and tell him that I agree. I agree one hundred per cent.*

LUTHER   *I have already told him that.*

(Night. MALCOLM and SIDNEY driving, on a country road, not far from MALCOLM's home. SIDNEY is driving.)

MALCOLM   *What is it you had to tell me—all alone?*

SIDNEY   *It's not easy to tell. I never believed it would come to this.* (He stops the car. MALCOLM looks wonderingly about him.) *Don't worry, Malcolm. I'm not going to kill you.* (MALCOLM looks at him.) *I never told you—but I used to be pretty good at demolition work. I guess I still am.* (Switches on his ignition, switches it off.) *I can make a small bomb and put it under the hood of your car—a small bomb, but powerful enough to blow your head off, once you turn the key.* (Again, switches the ignition on and off.) *The other day, I was asked to make such a bomb and put it under the hood of your car. I said I would.*

MALCOLM   *You said you would?*

(There are tears in SIDNEY's eyes when he looks at MALCOLM.)

SIDNEY   *Yes. I said I would, so they wouldn't ask anybody else to do it. And to give me time to warn you.*

MALCOLM   *To warn me of what?*

SIDNEY   *The word's out, Malcolm. They're saying that if we knew what you'd done, we'd be glad to kill you ourselves.*

MALCOLM   *Who asked you—to—*put a bomb in my car?

SIDNEY   *I wasn't exactly asked, I was told. I'm one of Allah's servants, too.*

MALCOLM   *Who told you to do it?*

SIDNEY   *The point is, they're going to get somebody else to try—*

MALCOLM   *Who told you, who told you, who told you to do it!*

SIDNEY   *Malcolm. Don't make me say it.*

(MALCOLM *slumps back.*)

MALCOLM   *Why? I've given my life to The Movement.*

SIDNEY   *You think other people are like you. They're not like you.—I guess I've known—for a long time —but I didn't want to tell you. I couldn't.*

MALCOLM   *I can't believe that anybody in The Movement would want my death. What for? What have I done?*

SIDNEY   *I think that when my father met you in prison, Malcolm, he really loved you. You were like a son to him. You always say that he saved your life in prison—but you saved his life, too. He had someone who looked up to him, someone who listened to him, someone—he was able to convert. But he never dreamed that you'd become what you've become. And he's been worried about you and jealous of you, oh, for a long time now.*

MALCOLM   *He wasn't like that in prison. How can people change so much?*

SIDNEY   *Maybe he was like that in prison. He was always the king-pin, remember? He ruled. He judged
others. They didn't judge him. And he'd be the
king-pin in The Movement if it weren't for you. We
give a rally, eight thousand people aren't going to
come out and hear him. But they'll come out to hear
you.*

(He starts the car. They begin moving.)

MALCOLM   *Sidney, I can't make any sense out of it. I
haven't done any of this for myself. I revere the
Honorable Messenger above all men on earth. I love
your father more than I love myself, and I've always trusted him, not only with my life, but with the
lives of my wife and children. Now, I don't know—
I don't know—why?*

SIDNEY   *Malcolm, The Movement is big and getting
bigger. Look. If you decided The Movement wasn't
what it was supposed to be, you'd leave and you'd
tell the people why. They don't want to risk that.
And if you stay with The Movement, well, the Honorable Messenger's old, he doesn't have any children. You only have daughters now, but you likely
to have sons. But my father—Luther—he's got sons
now!*

MALCOLM   *Is that what it's about? a dynasty! from the*

*nickels and dimes of poor black people!—I don't
believe you.*

SIDNEY   *You mean, you don't believe it's happening.
Neither do I.*

MALCOLM   *If they're really after me—what can I do?*

SIDNEY   *I've warned some other people, people I know
can be trusted. We just have to make it as hard for
them as possible.*

MALCOLM   *When they silenced me for ninety days, then
—they never meant to reinstate me.*

SIDNEY   *No. I knew that.*

MALCOLM   *Luther knew it all the time—?*

SIDNEY   *Malcolm—it's practically Luther's idea. He's
always made sure the Honorable Messenger didn't
trust you.*

MALCOLM   *How long have you known this?*

SIDNEY   *Now, it seems to me that I've known it for a
long time. It's hard to—he's my father, after all.*

MALCOLM   *Yes.—Poor Sidney.*

SIDNEY   *Poor you. Here. I've brought you safely home.*

MALCOLM   *So you have. Thank you Sidney.*

SIDNEY   *As-Salaam-Alaikum.*

MALCOLM   *Wa-Alaikum-Salaam.*

(MALCOLM steps out of the car. SIDNEY drives off.
MALCOLM fumbles with his keys, enters his house.
BETTY is standing in the living room. They stare at
each other a long moment.)

BETTY   *So, now you know.*

MALCOLM   *Yes. I know now.*

(He sits, abruptly, as though he has been struck.)

*I feel as though something in nature has failed. My
head—my head feels as though it's going to burst.*

(BETTY watches him, walks over to him, and holds
his head against her breasts.)

(Night. MALCOLM and BETTY, in bed.)

BETTY   *What are you going to do?*

215

MALCOLM   *I don't know yet.—It's as though I'm married to you, and I think it's a fine, happy marriage. And then, one morning, without any warning, you shove some divorce papers across the table at me. Well. You can get a divorce legally, that's easy. But, then, to really be divorced, psychologically divorced—that can take years.—Before I married The Movement, I didn't have any life—and now—*

BETTY   *The Movement gave you life, but you gave life to The Movement, too, Malcolm. Remember that.*

MALCOLM   *I feel like someone who doesn't even have anything to remember any more. When I was a hustler out there in those streets, the worst thing that could happen to you was for someone to set you up as a dupe, as a chump—like Luther's done to me!*

BETTY   *The people still trust you, Malcolm. There are a whole lot of folks out there just waiting for you to say the word—and they'll follow you.*

MALCOLM   *I feel like such a child now—such a fool— I don't know if I'm fit to ask anybody to follow me.*

BETTY   *Malcolm—you're going to have to do it. You might as well make up your mind to that.*

MALCOLM   *I have to find out if it's true—if it's true!*

(Close-Up: MALCOLM.)

MALCOLM   *I am not here to plead for me, but to bring
up a very important matter which I never had the
courage to bring up to you before.*

(Pull Back: to reveal MALCOLM and LUTHER, in LU-
THER's study. It is late afternoon.
LUTHER watches MALCOLM steadily.)

*It's been on my mind for months. Every time
I faced an audience, I was scared inside that someone would bring up the question—*

LUTHER   *The question of my adultery?*

MALCOLM   *Yes.*

LUTHER   *Why has it worried you so?*

MALCOLM   *Luther, we taught the people to be chaste.
We said the marriage vows were holy—that their
bodies were sacred. We were trying to undo the
damage caused our people by four hundred years
of the white man's slave morality. And now, you—
a minister—how can you betray—the people?*

LUTHER   *I am not accused of rape, Malcolm. Women
like power.*

217

MALCOLM   *You sound like somebody—I used to know.*

LUTHER   *You're being childish, Malcolm. The people aren't upset. The Movement—The Movement which you really think is your Movement!—isn't menaced. The people are wiser than you, Malcolm, and they know that all human beings are fallible. They expect their leaders to be fallible. Otherwise, they couldn't relate to them at all.—King David is still King David, even though he slept with Bathsheba, and murdered many men. People don't remember that. They remember King David, who wrote the Psalms. People don't remember Noah's drunkenness and nakedness. They remember that he built the ark. People know what you don't know, Malcolm— what's written is written. Who are you to change that? Who do you think you are?*

MALCOLM   *I think I'm a servant of Allah. I think I've served The Movement well. It's been my life, my soul, dearer to me than my own flesh and blood—I never dreamed—I think I'm Malcolm X.*

LUTHER   *Well. You owe that to me. So, take my advice, now, and cool off.*

MALCOLM   *What did you say?*

LUTHER   *I said, take my advice, and cool off.*

MALCOLM   *No. Before that.*

LUTHER   *I said—you said you were Malcolm X. And I said—that you might not be that—if it hadn't been for me.*

MALCOLM   *No. That isn't what you said. You said, I owe it to you.*

LUTHER   *Well—don't you? Think back. It wasn't so very long ago.*

MALCOLM   *It was a very long time ago. You know what I think, Luther? You know what I'm beginning to think? You picked me up, sure—out of the mud. But, more and more, I'm beginning to think—I picked you up, too. I don't know what would have happened to me if it hadn't been for you. (Pauses, and looks at LUTHER.) But I don't know what would have happened to you, if it hadn't been for me. (He walks up and down.) You wouldn't be wearing that suit, would you, Luther?—How blind I've been! Or that watch. You wouldn't be in this house —with those heavy drapes over your windows, so you won't hear the howling in the streets outside. Would you, Luther? Is that what it was, for you?*

LUTHER   *Stop being so emotional. One hand washes the other.*

(MALCOLM walks to the window.)

MALCOLM   *Who washes them? I thought it was for them, Luther. I thought it was for boys like the boy I used to be. I thought it was for men like the man I thought you were. I thought it was for girls—like girls I used to know—and women like my mother. I thought—we were* trying to save a nation. *Oh, Luther. I wasn't trying to wash my hands. I wanted the people to find out who they were, and be proud of who they were. I thought it was for that.*

LUTHER   *It* is for that. *You just don't know who the people are. You think they're like you. They're not like you.*

MALCOLM   *Am I in any danger?*

LUTHER   *What kind of danger?*

MALCOLM   *Danger.*

LUTHER   *Go home and get some sleep. You must be very tired.*

MALCOLM   *Yes, I am—Luther?*

LUTHER   *Yes?*

MALCOLM   *If I were in danger—and you knew it—would you tell me?*

LUTHER   *I told you. One hand washes the other.*

MALCOLM   *So you did. Peace, brother.*

LUTHER   *Peace.*

(Day. The Hotel Theresa. A press conference. BETTY is sitting far in the rear.

Pan from BETTY forward to MALCOLM, as MALCOLM speaks.)

MALCOLM   *I am going to organize and head a new mosque in New York City known as The Muslim Mosque, Inc. This will give us a religious base, and the spiritual force necessary to rid our people of the vices that destroy the moral fiber of our community.* (Close-up: SIDNEY, sitting very near the front, watching and watchful. MALCOLM: frightened, but determined.) *We will have our temporary headquarters in the Hotel Theresa, in Harlem. It will be the working base for an action program designed to eliminate the political oppression—*(MALCOLM's point of view: flash-bulbs flashing, black and white faces in and out of focus.)*—the economic exploitation, and the social degradation suffered daily by twenty-two million Afro-Americans.*

(Morning. SIDNEY's hand snaps shut a suitcase, bearing the initials: MX.

Traveling shot: the suitcase, initials prominent, being carried outdoors.

Close-up: BETTY, facing a mirror, fixing a white headband around her head. Her face is very thoughtful.

MALCOLM enters the room, dressed for travel.)

MALCOLM   *You ready?*

BETTY   *Yes.*

MALCOLM   *I know this journey isn't very practical. But I know you know why I must make it.*

BETTY   *I want you to make this journey.*

MALCOLM   *I may never be able to pay my sister back. I know I'm not being practical. But I hope you don't think I'm being foolish.*

BETTY   *You're no more practical and no more foolish than you were the day we met, or the day we married. I told you, the first time I ever saw you—I thought you were too young to be so serious. You were doing like you doing now—wiping your glasses.*

MALCOLM   *I must go to the source—*

BETTY   *I knew that, then.*

MALCOLM   *When I come back from Mecca, I promise you—I promise—that we'll never be separated for such long periods again. We'll get someone to take care of the children, and we'll travel together.*

BETTY   *I would love that. But you mustn't worry about it. For me—you are present when you are away.*

(He embraces her: a long moment.)

MALCOLM   *I guess I will say bye now: I love you, Betty.*

BETTY   *I love you.*

ATILAH'S VOICE   *Mama? Daddy? We're waiting.*

(BETTY and MALCOLM smile at each other.)

BETTY   *It's your daughter. When she's ready, she expects everybody to be ready.*

MALCOLM   *We'll be right there.* (To BETTY) *This is the only way for me to know—if I'm fit to be a leader.*

(Close-up: SIDNEY's hands, putting MALCOLM's suitcase, initials prominent, into the trunk of the car.

223

SIDNEY's somewhat harried, watchful face, scanning the road.

The CHILDREN in the back seat.

The CHILDREN's point of view, through the car window:

MALCOLM, carrying his attaché case, following BETTY, comes out of the house.

MALCOLM locks the doors.

BETTY gets into the back seat, with the CHILDREN.

SIDNEY gets in, and slams the doors, and MALCOLM gets in.)

SIDNEY   *I been hoping you wouldn't change your mind.*

MALCOLM   *Brother Sidney, the white devil says you got about fifty horses under this hood. Now, how come you can't get this chariot to roll?*

SIDNEY   *Yes, suh, boss. Only too please to whip them horses, boss.*

(He switches on the ignition, and the car moves off.)

(Day. The observation tower, at Kennedy airport.

BETTY's point of view: people crossing the field toward the Lufthansa plane.

Pan: the CHILDREN's faces.

Close-up: BETTY. Her eyes are searching for MAL-
COLM.

Close-up: SIDNEY.)

SIDNEY *There he is.*

(MALCOLM, walking. He reaches the plane steps,
pauses, and looks behind him.

BETTY and SIDNEY wave.

The CHILDREN wave and call.

Close-up: MALCOLM. He does not see them yet.

The CHILDREN call: Daddy! Daddy!

BETTY takes her white headband from her head and
waves it like a banner.

Close-up: MALCOLM, starting up the steps.

He sees BETTY's banner, and his face changes. He
waves and smiles.

Close-up: the banner, flying.

Close-up: MALCOLM.

He is looking backward, slowly ascending. Then,
he is at the door, and the shadow of the interior falls
over his face.

He waves one last time, hands the stewardess his
boarding pass, and disappears.

Close-up: BETTY, smiling, weeping.

Close-up: SIDNEY, grave.

Pan: the CHILDREN's wondering faces.

BETTY waves the banner.

Close-up: the banner, waving.

225

From the air: the Egyptian flag.

In the plane, MALCOLM's seat companion, a young, wealthy Egyptian, is speaking to MALCOLM. It is clear that they have been talking for hours.)

THE EGYPTIAN   —so that is all, the only thing that we in the East find dubious about your Movement. Islam teaches that all men are brothers, his color does not matter. White can be Muslim, as well as black, brown, and yellow.

MALCOLM   I understand you. It's just different in the United States. I don't know if I can explain it—

THE EGYPTIAN   Oh, no one can explain your country, no one. It is a most bizarre place, very backward. (MALCOLM laughs.) You laugh, but it is true. From the point of view of things human—very backward. —We are coming down now. Have you been to Egypt before?

MALCOLM   No, never.

THE EGYPTIAN   I hope you will like it. It is not like your country. We are backward in different ways than you. Just the same, we are the most industrialized nation in Africa. That is why the Western powers look on us with such suspicion. We are an example of what dark people can do. The English, espe-

cially, will never forgive our impertinence.—Do you know anyone in Cairo?

MALCOLM *Not really. I have a letter to the son of an Egyptian writer I know a little, in New York— Muhammad Shawarbi. He's studying at Cairo University.*

THE EGYPTIAN *Oh, he will be very happy to meet you. You are a kind of hero here for the young people —you and Cassius Clay.*

MALCOLM *That's why the Western powers look on us with such suspicion.*

(They laugh.)

THE EGYPTIAN *I am meeting a party of pilgrims here, friends of mine. Just a few of us. We are going to Jedda together. It would make me very happy if you would be one of our party.*

MALCOLM *I would be very happy. Very honored. Thank you very much.*

THE EGYPTIAN *It is nothing. You are my brother.*

(Traveling shot: the indescribable human press and confusion at the Cairo airport. Muslims of all colors under heaven, and all conditions, effusively, lovingly, greeting each other. Children are very prominent.

MALCOLM is being guided through this maelstrom by THE EGYPTIAN, who seems perfectly at home in this vortex, and delighted to be at home.

MALCOLM is astounded and delighted, like a child. THE EGYPTIAN watches him with affectionate amusement.)

THE EGYPTIAN *Very like your rush hour in Times Square, yes?*

MALCOLM *I never saw any hugging and kissing going on in Times Square. They'd throw you in jail, or in the loony-bin.*

THE EGYPTIAN *The Americans do seem to take a dim view of human contact.* (They have reached the baggage counter, where confusion reigns.) *If I may advise you, my brother—I would leave nearly all my luggage in Cairo. We try to make the pilgrimage as lightly burdened as possible. May I advise you?*

MALCOLM *I would be very grateful.*

THE EGYPTIAN *But there is no need. I am your brother.*

(Interior: an Egyptian luggage store. MALCOLM has just selected a small valise.)

THE EGYPTIAN *That is suitable, I think. That will carry one suit and some underwear, a pair of shoes—you will not need more, I think? And you will bring one camera.*

(Day. Interior: THE EGYPTIAN's home.)

THE EGYPTIAN *I will show you how we dress for our journey. We do this in order to enter into a state of spiritual and physical consecration. You will do as I do?*

(Solemnly, he begins to undress. After a moment, MALCOLM follows suit.

Jump-shot: THE EGYPTIAN, naked, stands in the middle of the room, draping a towel around his waist.)

THE EGYPTIAN *We call this the Isar.* (MALCOLM drapes his towel in the same way. THE EGYPTIAN throws another towel over his neck and shoulders.) *We call this the Rida.* (MALCOLM does as THE EGYPTIAN does.) *Our sandals*—(Steps into them, as does MAL- COLM.)—*and the money belt around the waist*— (He picks up a bag with a long strap, hands it to MALCOLM, takes another for himself.)—*into this go all our important papers. This was not so im- portant long ago—but now we must respect pass- ports and frontiers. How I long for the day when these obstacles to freedom become obsolete.* (He surveys MALCOLM.) *So—my brother. Now we are ready for our pilgrimage.*

(The Cairo airport. Thousands and thousands of pilgrims, all dressed exactly as MALCOLM is dressed.)

MALCOLM *You could be a king or a peasant—or anything—nobody would know.*

THE EGYPTIAN *That is why the Christians refer to us as heathens.*

(Interior: the plane, full of pilgrims, who are shouting one word over and over: "*Labbayka!*")

THE EGYPTIAN *Labbayka: here I come, O Lord.*

(Close-up: MALCOLM.)

MALCOLM *Here I come, O Lord. Labbayka. Labbayka.*

(The plane lands, and the pilgrims begin to descend.

Close-up: MALCOLM: terribly moved, blindly apprehensive, being carried both into and out of himself.

As he stands, the camera moves behind him so that only his head, neck, and shoulders are in the frame. Since he is nearly naked, he looks terribly vulnerable.

Very tight on MALCOLM's neck and shoulders, we

walk behind him to the door of the plane, and stand there with him, looking down.

MALCOLM's point of view: the astounding, multi-colored press of pilgrims, all united under Allah.

We slowly follow behind MALCOLM into the tremendous multitude.

MALCOLM and THE EGYPTIAN before the CUSTOMS CLERK.

The CUSTOMS CLERK holds MALCOLM's passport in his hand. Many people are speaking, in many languages at once—and all of it is about MALCOLM, who understands not a word. The CUSTOMS CLERK and THE EGYPTIAN speak together in Arabic. The CUSTOMS CLERK is obviously explaining something, and THE EGYPTIAN seems finally to understand what must be done.

THE EGYPTIAN thanks the CLERK, and turns back to MALCOLM.)

THE EGYPTIAN *My friend, people in this part of the world are prepared to believe that America can produce popcorn and automobiles and television sets and astronauts. They do not believe that America can produce a Muslim. It is not that he doubts you, or the friend who wrote the letter for you. It is that he cannot take it upon himself to allow you into Mecca. You must appear before the Muslim High Court. They will decide if you are a true Muslim or not. That is the law and there is nothing anyone can do about it.*

MALCOLM   *When can I appear before the court?*

THE EGYPTIAN   *Today is Friday. Friday is for Muslims what Sunday is supposed to be for Christians. Nothing is open today. You will have to wait until tomorrow, at least, and possibly even until Monday. I am very, very sorry. I would even wait with you if I could, but I cannot leave my friends.*

MALCOLM   *Don't worry. I'll be fine. Allah guides me.*

THE EGYPTIAN   *He certainly did not bring you so close to Mecca merely to lock the gates in your face. You see, I, in any case, believe in you. I did not tell you before, but I am something of an admirer of yours —and more than ever, now. It is not only black people in your country who depend on you. Many of us do, all over the world. And not only black people. Remember that.*

MALCOLM   *I will. Thank you.*

THE EGYPTIAN   *I am sorry I will not be privileged to be with you when you first enter Mecca. But it was a privilege to be your traveling companion. I must leave you now. Is there anything I can do for you before I leave?*

MALCOLM   *No. I thank you. You have done more than enough.*

THE EGYPTIAN *Peace be with you.*

MALCOLM *And unto you be peace.*

(They shake hands, and THE EGYPTIAN goes.

MALCOLM is frightened and downcast.

He starts walking through the crowded Jedda airport.

A Muslim woman puts a tablecloth over the Muslim rug.

She begins putting dishes of food on this rug: it is now a dining-room table.

A Muslim family is seated on the rug, talking: it is now a living room.

Another group of Muslims: an elderly Muslim is seated alone on the rug, talking, and the younger Muslims are gathered around: the rug is now a courtroom.

A Muslim family fast asleep on the rug: which is now a bedroom.

MALCOLM walks out of the airport.

He sees an open marketplace, where people are buying food.

He watches a man buy a roasted chicken, and begin to eat it.

He approaches the marketplace hesitantly, points to the chicken.

The proprietor, with a big smile, holds the chicken out to him.

MALCOLM holds out some money. The proprietor carefully selects several coins.

MALCOLM puts his change away, and begins tearing the chicken apart. One gets the impression that chicken has never tasted so good before.

MALCOLM has finished the chicken, and is again walking through the airport.

As he passes the CUSTOMS CLERK, he hears the phone ring, and the CLERK picks up the receiver.

MALCOLM stops, struck by a sudden thought.

He looks in the bag he is carrying, finds his wallet, looks through it, finds a slip of paper.

He walks over to the CLERK, waving the paper.)

MALCOLM- *Telephone?* (Jabbing the paper with his forefinger.) *Telephone. Friend.* (Pointing to the telephone.) *Friend. Friend.*

(It has taken him no time to gather a crowd. Others begin to translate for him, none in any language that MALCOLM understands.

The CLERK finally looks down at the paper. He seems impressed.)

CLERK *Friend? You?*

MALCOLM *Yes. Telephone. Telephone.*

CLERK *Telephone?*

MALCOLM   *Yes. Telephone.*

(The CLERK slowly begins to dial the number.
The other pilgrims register satisfaction.
The CLERK speaks into the phone, hands the phone
to MALCOLM.)

MALCOLM   *Hello? Dr. Azzam? You don't know me, but
my name is Malcolm X, from America. A friend of
your father's, sir, in New York, Dr. Shawarbi, gave
me your father's book and he gave me your phone
number—I am at the airport, sir, I wasn't allowed
to go on to Mecca—*

(Fade to an official-looking limousine pushing
through the crowds.
The pilgrims, who have taken a proprietary interest
in MALCOLM, cheer him into this car.)

(Morning. The Muslim High Court. The examination is over.
Close-up: MALCOLM's name being inscribed in the
Holy Register of True Muslims: *El-Haji Malik El
Shabazz*.
Night. From within the limousine, MALCOLM's point
of view: the car makes a tortuous progress through narrow, winding, ancient streets, shops, bazaars, tens of
thousands of pilgrims.

The car stops at some distance from the Great Mosque.

MALCOLM'S GUIDE, a tall black man in long white robes, takes off his shoes, and MALCOLM does the same.

They perform their ablutions before the Mosque, and enter.

The Ka'aba, a great black stone house in the middle of the Mosque, is being "circumambulated by thousands and thousands of praying pilgrims, of both sexes, and every size, shape, and color in the world."

Close-up: MALCOLM.)

MALCOLM *O Lord, you are peace and peace derives from you. So greet us, O Lord, with peace.* (He cannot get close enough to the Ka'aba to touch it, to kiss it, as other pilgrims are doing. Therefore, he raises his hands, along with thousands of others, and shouts as they shout.) *Takbir! Takbir! God is great. God is great.*

(MALCOLM moves with other pilgrims seven times around the Ka'aba, and prostrates himself.)

(Day: the sun rising over Mount Arafat.

MALCOLM moves alone among the great host of pilgrims. The light of the sun is as nothing compared to the great light on his face.

Facing the sun, he kneels and prays.

Night. MALCOLM, alone in his hotel room.

The windows are open; we hear the sounds of Muslim celebrations.

MALCOLM is very peaceful. He is writing a letter.)

MALCOLM'S VOICE OVER *Throughout my travels in the Muslim world, I have met, talked to, and even eaten with people who, in America, would have been considered white—I have never before seen* true *and* sincere *brotherhood practiced by all colors together, irrespective of their color.*

(Close-up: BETTY, reading alone in their house, at night.)

MALCOLM'S VOICE OVER *You may be shocked by these words coming from me. I have eaten from the same plate, drunk from the same glass, and slept in the same bed (or on the same rug) while praying to the same God—with fellow Muslims, whose eyes were the bluest of blue, whose hair was the blondest of blond, and whose skin was the whitest of white. We were truly the same—brothers!—because their belief in one God had removed the "white" from their minds, the "white" from their behavior, and the "white" from their attitude. In the past, yes, I have made sweeping indictments of all white people. I never will be guilty of that again. —The true Islam has shown me that a blanket indictment of all white people is as wrong as when*

*whites make blanket indictments against blacks.
Yes, I have been convinced that some American
whites do want to help cure the rampant racism
which is on the path to destroying this country.—I
have been asked to visit Lagos, and Accra—*

(BETTY walks slowly into the bedroom, and leans over the children's bed.)

(Day. MALCOLM, addressing the Nigerian Muslim Students Society. The hall is packed. He is reaching his peroration.)

MALCOLM   —*The world's course will change the day
the African heritage peoples come together as
brothers! The slaughter of black people in South
Africa and the slaughter of black people in Ala-
bama, or, for that matter, in New York, is the same
slaughter, and it will not end until nonwhite peoples all over the world consider themselves as one.
It is the only answer to the old British policy, which
she is using until today, called: divide and rule!*

(Pan: the cheering African faces.
Close-up: an African STUDENT.)

STUDENT   *We wish to make you an honorary member of
the Nigerian Muslim Students Society, sir. And we
have given you a new name, in the Yoruba lan-*

guage. It is Omowale. It means: the son who has
come home.

(MALCOLM, at the University of Ghana's Great
Hall. It is packed, mostly with Africans, but also present
are Americans, white and black.)

MALCOLM   *—until you expose the man in Washington,*
D.C., you haven't accomplished anything. Ameri-
can agents have been following me everywhere I've
been, and they are in this audience tonight. And
they're not here to offer me a job working for the
USIS. (Laughter, mostly black.) *I know that my*
government will tell you that the black man's situa-
tion in America is improving all the time. Don't be-
lieve them. That's just another tactic to keep us con-
fused and divided. And you know something? I've
never seen so many whites so nice to so many blacks
as you white people here in Africa. In America,
Afro-Americans are struggling for integration.
They should come here—to Africa—to see how
you grin at Africans. You've really got integration
here. But can you tell the Africans that in America
you grin at black people? No, you can't! And you
don't honestly like these Africans any better, either
—but what you do *like is the* minerals *Africa has*
under her soil. (Pan: the faces, black and white,
most of the whites uneasy and angry, some thoughtful.) *I'm not anti-American, and I didn't come here*

*to condemn America—I want to make that very
clear! I came here to tell the truth—and if the truth
condemns America, then she stands condemned!*

(Night. Music. The Press Club. A great party.
Ghanaians dancing the High Life.

MALCOLM is talking to a small group of African
students, male and female.)

MALCOLM *You wonder why I don't dance? Because I
want you to remember the twenty-two million Afro-
Americans in the US!*

FEMALE STUDENT *You must be the bridge between us.
You must tell them—that our struggle here, your
struggle there—it is the same.*

MALE STUDENT *And you must come back to us. You
must come back to us soon.*

(Close-up: MALCOLM. He touches his beard, smiles
—but is suddenly very far away, looking at something
only he can see.)

MALCOLM *Ins'allah. God willing.*

(Exterior: day. MALCOLM's car, and behind it, a
great procession of dancing, singing, cheering Africans.

The airport. Pan: the faces—shouting good-bye, waving good-bye.

Close-up: MALCOLM, on the airplane steps, very moved, waving.

Close-up: the wheels of the plane: beginning to roll.

Close-up: the nose of the plane: as it moves toward us.

Pan: the African faces: sober and thoughtful now.

From the plane window, MALCOLM's point of view: the plane begins to move, turns, and the silent mass of Africans is hidden from our view. The plane begins to race, lifts, hits the clouds.

Through the clouds, from the air: the American flag.

Flash-bulbs flashing, filling the screen, and a great cacophony of voices.

Close-up: BETTY.

Pull back, to reveal that BETTY is standing far in the back of the press room at Kennedy Airport, and MALCOLM is enduring a press conference.)

1ST WHITE REPORTER *Mr. Malcolm X, what about those Blood Brothers, reportedly affiliated with your organization, reportedly trained for violence, who have killed innocent white people?*

MALCOLM *Why don't you ever ask white people, who are trained for violence, about all the innocent black people they kill? When a white youth kills* somebody, that's a "sociological" problem. But when a black youth kills somebody, you want to start building gas ovens. Why is it you weren't worried when black people killed only each other? As long as black people were being murdered in cold blood, as long as black people were being lynched, you just said, "Things will get better."

2ND REPORTER   Mr. Malcolm X, what about your comment that Negroes should form rifle clubs?

MALCOLM   The Constitution gives you the right, as a white man, to have a rifle in your home. The Constitution gives you the right to protect yourself. Why is it "ominous" when black people even talk of having rifles? Why don't we have the right to self-defense? Is it because maybe you know we're going to have to defend ourselves against you?

3RD REPORTER   Mr. Malcolm X, don't you think there's been any progress at all in civil rights?

MALCOLM   Why should a citizen have to fight for his civil rights? Why should I have to fight for what you were born with? No! To keep the American black man on his knees, begging for his civil rights, is a trap. It's a way of keeping black people from realizing that they have a strong, airtight case to bring the United States before the United Nations

*on a formal accusation of a denial of human rights
—and if Angola and South Africa could be cen-
sured, there is no way for the United States to es-
cape censure, right on its home ground!*

4TH REPORTER   *Mr. Malcolm X, what about your letter
from Mecca? Didn't you say that you now accept
white men as brothers?*

MALCOLM   *I hope that once and for all, my Hajj to the
Holy City of Mecca has established our Muslim
Mosque's authentic religious affiliation with the
seven hundred and fifty million Muslims of the
orthodox Islamic world. And I know once and for
all that the Black Africans look upon America's
twenty-two million blacks as long lost brothers! Just
as I wrote, I shared true brotherly love with many
white-complexioned Muslims who never gave a single thought to the race, or to the complexion, of another Muslim. In two weeks in the Holy Land, I
saw what I never had seen in thirty-nine years here
in America. I saw all races, all colors—blue-eyed
blonds to black-skinned Africans—in true brother-
hood! In unity! Living as one! Worshipping as one!
And now that I am back in America, my attitude
here concerning white people has to be governed by
what my black brothers and I experience here and
what we witness here—in terms of brotherhood.
White people have believed for so long that they*

were in some way superior that they may never be able to overcome that sickness. I'll tell you this: our African brothers are happy to know that we are waking from our long sleep—after so-called Christian white America had taught us to be ashamed of our African brothers and homeland!—And now, if you'll excuse me, gentlemen, I'd like to join my patient wife, and go home.

(Close-up: BETTY, smiling.)

(Exterior. Night. The Audubon Ballroom, in Harlem. A poster, advertising MALCOLM X, which says that the public is invited.

Traveling shot: into the hall, packed, predominantly black. The white press is there, and so are policemen—surly, distrustful, and quiet.

MALCOLM is speaking.)

MALCOLM   —*not Muslim, nor Christian, Catholic nor Protestant, Baptist nor Methodist, Democrat nor Republican, Mason nor Elk!* (Pan: the attentive, somewhat bewildered faces.) *I mean the black people of America—and the black people all over this earth. Because it is as this collective mass of black people that we have been deprived not only of our civil rights, but even our human rights, the right to human dignity—*

244

(Interior. Night. A Harlem bar.

Not very crowded, dimly lit: about four or five men sitting at the bar, among them one or two "do-rag" brothers.)

BARMAID   *Something sure must have happened to him over yonder in them holy lands. I don't know what he's trying to say. Do you know what he's trying to say?*

1ST CUSTOMER   *I'll be damned.*

2ND CUSTOMER   *I don't think he knows.*

3RD CUSTOMER   *Look. Somebody got to him and give him some bread. Shit. That's what always happens. How did he get over there, in the first place? You got the bread to go to Africa?*

1ST CUSTOMER   *I sure as hell don't. Can't hardly make it to Atlantic City.*

2ND CUSTOMER   *Well, then.*

BARMAID   *I ain't about to shake hands with no white man, I know that. Shit. It's dangerous.*

1ST CUSTOMER   *All white men is all born cops. And all born cops is born criminals.*

BARMAID   *Don't tell* me. *I'll tell* you.

4TH CUSTOMER (elderly)   *I'll tell you something, I've seen it happen. That boy's mind's been clouded ever since he left the Honorable Messenger, and went out on his own. He didn't have no business doing that. He ain't no prophet. And when you go against a prophet, man, I'm telling you—you better watch out.*

2ND CUSTOMER   *Well, I'll be damned. Listen to the old preacher.*

SIDNEY'S VOICE   *He's right. That's what happened.*

(Pan: as the faces turn, to SIDNEY, who has been sitting alone at the end of the bar. He is weary, disheveled, and a little drunk.)

SIDNEY   *There was just one trouble with Brother Malcolm. He couldn't accept discipline. He always thought he was right. And that's why he had to leave The Movement. Can't have nobody like that in no Movement. They just fuck everything up.*

BARMAID   *Do you know him?*

SIDNEY   *Damn right, I used to know him.*

BARMAID   *You don't know him no more?*

SIDNEY   *Not since he left The Movement.*

BARMAID   *You in The Movement? You don't look like you in no Movement.*

SIDNEY   *No. I'm not in no Movement.—The man just couldn't accept discipline. Why, if I'm part of a revolutionary movement, and somebody orders me to kill somebody, why, I'm supposed to do it, that's all. That's revolution. That's discipline. And discipline is the black man's only hope.*

BARMAID   *Well—ain't no need to cry about it.*

SIDNEY (rises)   *Discipline, sister! Discipline!*

(And he leaves the bar.)

(Interior. Day. MALCOLM is sitting in the bleak waiting room of The Tombs. An elderly black woman and a young Puerto Rican girl sit near him.

The GUARD comes to the door.)

GUARD   *Mr. X—?*

(MALCOLM rises and follows the GUARD. They are facing the great, barred prison gate. MALCOLM hands the GUARD his visitor's slip and the GUARD unlocks the gate.

MALCOLM is led to a small room, with a glass partition.

Long shot: SIDNEY being led through the prison corridor.

Close-up: SIDNEY, sitting down on the other side of the partition.

He looks at MALCOLM with a small, sullen smile.)

MALCOLM   *How are you, brother?*

SIDNEY   *How did you know I was here?*

MALCOLM   *It was in the papers.*

SIDNEY   *I guess my father doesn't read the papers.*

MALCOLM   *What in the world made you think that you were cut out for armed robbery?*

SIDNEY   *Maybe I didn't know what else I was cut out for. People change, Malcolm. You ought to know that.*

MALCOLM   *I don't know if I know what you mean.*

SIDNEY   *I don't mean anything, forget it.*

248

MALCOLM   *Betty told me when I came home that you'd dropped out of sight, stopped coming by—that you seemed to be mad at me about something. What have I done, Sidney?*

SIDNEY   *When you went away from here, you were a firebrand, you were something else! I loved you. I trusted you. I put down my own father to go with you. I thought we could start to change this whole filthy system. That's what I thought. And what do you do? You go across the pond and they give you some champagne and some dancing girls and before you even get back, you start sounding like some old Baptist preacher, talking about loving the white man and all that crap! It made me sick—you make me sick!*

MALCOLM   *Sidney—that isn't what I said.*

SIDNEY   *No? That's what a whole lot of people heard— and it made them sick, too.*

MALCOLM   *Sidney, I'm trying to turn a corner—*

SIDNEY   *Into the White House?*

MALCOLM   *Look. What I tried to say about true brother-hood in the Muslim world is true. But I never said it was true here. But there are some white people*

*here as dedicated to change as—as—as I am. I
didn't say there were very many—in fact, I've said
exactly the opposite. But maybe, you know, there
are never very many people, no matter what their
color, who are dedicated to change.*

SIDNEY   *Oh, Malcolm, Malcolm, what's come over you?
I can take you through this prison right now, and
show you a thousand black men dedicated to
change! Waiting for someone to help them to change
things! For help—they need help! You know who's
in these prisons? Niggers and Puerto Ricans, niggers and Puerto Ricans. And they in here because
ain't no other place for them in this fucked-up white
man's society—and I'm supposed to love this man?
Shit. I wish I really was a cannibal, like they say we
are. I'd fix me a missionary stew, baby—and eat for
days.*

MALCOLM   *I know who's in prison—and I know why.
I was in prison, too, and I remember it, even though
I think you think I don't . All I've been trying to say
is that white people in this country are what they are
not because of the color of their skins—they're what
they are because of this country—because they live
in a racist country. I've been trying to say what I'm
beginning to see—Christianity and capitalism are
the two evils which have placed us where we are—
in prison.*

250

SIDNEY   *The white man brought us here, baby, to make money off our flesh. And now that he don't need us to make money for him no more, he's going to get rid of us. It's as cold as that. This ain't no prison. It's a dress rehearsal for a concentration camp!*

MALCOLM   *How can I make you believe me again?*

SIDNEY   *By getting us out of prison.*

(Knocks for the GUARD, rises, leaves.)

(Interior. Evening. LUTHER's house.
We follow a handsome, tall black man in to LU-THER's study.)

MAN   *Mr. Malcolm X to see you.*

LUTHER   *Malcolm X?* (The MAN nods.) *Show him in. But make sure you search him first.*

(Close-up: MALCOLM, as he is being searched. A wry smile touches his lips.
The MAN escorts him into LUTHER's study. They are left alone there.
They watch each other a moment.)

LUTHER   *Sit down.*

251

(MALCOLM sits. He sees that LUTHER is leaving it up to him to begin the conversation.)

MALCOLM   *I went to see your son today—in prison.*

LUTHER   *Did you? I haven't seen Sidney in some time —about six months, I'd say.*

MALCOLM   *You don't seem to care much about what's happened to him.*

LUTHER   *Sidney left me to join you. I knew what would happen to him. It happens to everyone who leaves the Honorable Messenger. Their minds become clouded. They are cursed. Sidney is no longer my son. He is dead for me—you should know that. That's why there has been no communication between us. There has been no communication between you and me, either—so what are you doing here now?*

MALCOLM   *I had to see you. There were questions I wanted to ask you.*

LUTHER   *Questions? It was a very long time ago that you ceased asking questions of me. It was you who became the teacher.—I can't spend very much time with you. The Honorable Messenger will be very*

*displeased to know that I have received you at all.
—Ask your questions.*

(MALCOLM *rises and walks to the door.*
Close-up: LUTHER: *tense and sad.*)

MALCOLM   *You and the Honorable Messenger see eye
to eye on everything?*

LUTHER   *Yes. We do. I'm happy to say.*

MALCOLM   *Including who dies—whether it's Sidney, or
me.*

LUTHER   *It isn't up to me whether Sidney lives or dies.
It isn't up to me whether you live or die. What's
written—is written.—I'd save you if I could—from
your own pride, your own folly!*

MALCOLM   *What's the difference between the black people who want me dead and the white people who
want me dead? Aren't they really the same people?
Aren't they really working together?*

LUTHER   *I don't know of anyone who wishes you dead.
Your mind is clouded. If harm comes to you, it will
be because of your foolish teaching and that pride
of yours which made you repudiate the prophet of
the Lord of all the worlds!*

MALCOLM *You've won, you know. What will you do now—with your power?*

LUTHER *I will keep it, and use it.*

MALCOLM *I thought you wanted to change the world.*

LUTHER *I know that's what you thought. Malcolm—the world's much more like me than it is like you. People recognize me. They see me in their mirror. But they don't hardly ever see you. You're not in the mirror with them. That's why people always look so—surprised—when they see you. You want to change them. I don't want to change them. And they —don't want to be changed.*

(Close-up: MALCOLM: as he turns to the window.
MALCOLM's point of view: the city streets.
These streets, briefly, become a kaleidoscope of his past.)

LOUISE'S VOICE *Don't let them feed that boy no pig.*

EARL'S VOICE *Our homeland is—in Africa!*

(SOPHIA and MALCOLM, dancing.)

MALCOLM *And what we going to do—when I come back here for you?*

SOPHIA *You seem to like music—and I've a radio in my car.*

(Close-up: LAURA)

LAURA *Oh, you could be a wonderful man, Malcolm.*

(Close-up: the latter-day LAURA.)

LAURA *My bitch would never go for it.*

THE EGYPTIAN *There is no need. You are my brother.*

BETTY *You are present when you are away.*

(The sun rising over Mount Arafat.
Close-up: MALCOLM: turning to face LUTHER.)

MALCOLM *I don't believe you. I know better. Like I know I'm better than you—I know people are better than that.*

LUTHER *I know you think so. Get home safely.*

(MALCOLM leaves. LUTHER walks to the window.)

(Interior. Night. BETTY, standing at the window of their house.
BETTY's point of view: a dark car, parked across the street.

MALCOLM's car comes down the block and parks in front of the house.

MALCOLM enters the house.

The dark car flashes on its headlights and drives away.

Interior. Evening. MALCOLM's house.

He comes to BETTY and puts his arms around her.)

MALCOLM   *Everything all right?*

BETTY   *Yes. Everything's all right.*

MALCOLM   *The girls are asleep?*

BETTY   *Yes. The girls are asleep.—You look tired. Go wash up. I'll get supper ready.*

MALCOLM   *The people don't believe in me any more. I've been trying to turn a corner—but every time I try, the old Malcolm X stands there, barring the way.*

BETTY   *Malcolm, I know it's hard on you. But you have to remember that it's hard on them. After all, you left the country. And when you left this country, you were able to see what you would never have seen if you stayed here. Dear heart: be patient. The people need you, and they love you, more than ever. If*

*they're a little bewildered—no one can blame them
for that.*

MALCOLM   *I don't want to do more harm than good.*

BETTY   *I can't do much for you these days, except feed
you. But I do have one advantage. I know who you
are better than you do. Wash up, and come and
try to eat.*

(*Night.* A Molotov cocktail fills the screen and
comes crashing through the window of MALCOLM's living
room, setting the house on fire.

MALCOLM and BETTY rise out of sleep at once, he
very calm, she much less so.)

MALCOLM   *Get the children! Get the children! Bring
them outside.* (She rushes to the children's bedroom. He rushes to the phone.) *Get me the fire department. The fire department!*

(Close-up: BETTY, assembling the children, and realizing that there is no time to dress them.)

BETTY   *Come on, now, come. Come along. Come.*

MALCOLM   *I want to report a fire—yes, it's burning
now, why else would I be calling you?—at the following address—*

BETTY   *Come on, now, come. Don't be frightened.*

(She gets the children onto the back porch. MAL-
COLM follows her.)

MALCOLM   *Are they all there?*

BETTY   *Yes.*

MALCOLM   *Count them.*

(BETTY, silently, touching the children's heads,
counts them.)

BETTY   *Yes, Malcolm. They're all here. But they're
cold. What are we going to do?*

MALCOLM   *Count them again.*

(The lights of a NEIGHBOR flash on. A male NEIGH-
BOR appears in his doorway.)

NEIGHBOR   *Brother Malcolm! Sister Betty! Come on
over here!* (MALCOLM picks up two of the children
and they start for the NEIGHBOR's house.) *Where
are the fire engines?*

(He puts down the children on the porch of the
NEIGHBOR's house. BETTY and the children enter the
house.

MALCOLM looks around him:
at the dark landscape.
the fire.
the sky.)

MALCOLM   *Where are the fire engines?*

(Insert: EARL LITTLE's house, burning.
the neighbors, watching.
the firemen, watching.
the face of LOUISE, watching.
the trolley-car tracks, as the trolley bears down on
EARL.)

NEIGHBOR   *Come inside, Brother Malcolm.*

MALCOLM (he is not speaking to the NEIGHBOR)   *Okay.*

(Exterior. Morning, before the ruined house: MAL-
COLM, *and the press.*)

MALCOLM   *I know. And I know what your newspapers
will make of it. I accuse The Movement of having
fire-bombed my house—and they accuse me—even
though my wife and children were sleeping in this
house—of having set this fire myself, to gain publicity for myself.*

(Interior. Day. The Tombs.

SIDNEY, and other prisoners, listening to this on the radio. Montage:

LAURA: in a bar, listening.

A white hand picks up a telephone receiver.

A black hand puts a telephone receiver down.

Close-up: SOPHIA: as she leans over to click the radio off.

Close-up: LUTHER: facing the press.)

LUTHER   *I think you gentlemen will agree with me;*
          The Movement can have no possible interest in fire-
          bombing property which we own.

(MALCOLM at an airport phone booth, talking.

Two white men appear. One stands quite far away, one approaches the booth.

Close-up: MALCOLM: terribly aware of these two men.

The man nearest the booth passes out of MALCOLM's line of vision.

Close-up: the harried MALCOLM: leaving the booth.
He starts walking.

Two black men begin to walk behind him.

MALCOLM finds his car in the parking lot, and gets into his car.

The two black men are still watching him.

Close-up: MALCOLM: as he starts to turn the ignition key: and stops.

Close-up: MALCOLM's eyes, in the rear-view mirror.

The two men have started walking toward him.

He turns the key, and starts the car.

Close-up: Betty.)

BETTY   *You know I never, never, never have tried to tell you what to do—I never have! But you can't go wandering around alone—you can't! Malcolm—that's all there is to it. You can't.*

MALCOLM   *Betty—you're all I have. I'll do as you say. Really, I will. But—it's not just The Movement that's after me. I know what they can do, I taught them—and I know what they can't do.*

(The telephone rings. They both stare at it. One of the children rushes in to answer it. BETTY, with the violence of terror, snatches the phone from the child's bewildered hands.)

BETTY   *Hello? Yes?—Oh. How are you, Brother Benjamin?*

(Close-up: MALCOLM: holding his child.)

BETTY   *Why, yes. Yes. Malcolm is here. Sunday, at the Audubon Ballroom. Yes. Yes. Would you like to talk to Malcolm?—All right, Brother Benjamin. We'll see you Sunday. Goodnight.* (BETTY puts down the receiver, and MALCOLM puts down the child. Over the child's head, they look at each other.) *That was just Brother Benjamin X. He just wanted to confirm your appearance at the Audubon Ballroom, Sunday night.*

MALCOLM   *Oh. Yes.*

BETTY   *Kiss your daddy goodnight, and go on back to bed.*

ATILAH   *Goodnight, Daddy.*

MALCOLM   *Goodnight.* (ATILAH *goes.*) *I don't think I want you and the children to come to the Audubon on Sunday. And, from now on, I think I'm going to make a point of staying in the city, whenever I have to speak there—of staying in the city the night before.*

(BETTY goes to him, and kisses him. They kiss long and hard.)

(Day. Exterior. A poster. saying that MALCOLM X is speaking, and that the public is invited, to the Audubon Ballroom.
    Exterior. Morning: from the air: the New York Hilton.
    Interior: the garage of the New York Hilton: empty and somber.

Interior: the Hilton lobby. Two black men enter, separately, one goes to a house phone, one sits down.

Interior: MALCOLM's room, at the Hilton. MALCOLM, asleep.

The telephone rings.

MALCOLM awakens, and picks up the receiver.

Close-up: MALCOLM.)

MALCOLM   *Hello—?*

A VOICE   *Wake up, Brother Malcolm.*

(We hear the *click*, as the VOICE hangs up.)

MALCOLM   *Wake up, Malcolm.* (He sits up in bed. There is a strange smile on his face.) *Wake up, Malcolm.* (He picks up the receiver.) *Hello—? Operator?—Operator, I want to call my wife. Her name is Mrs. Betty Shabazz. The number is—*

(Interior. Day. MALCOLM's house. The phone is ringing. BETTY runs to answer it.)

BETTY   *Hello?—Malcolm? Oh, good morning, dear heart. What? Well, you certainly change your mind fast enough—no, sweetheart, I don't mind. I'll get the children dressed. We'll be there.—Yes. Yes. Dear heart. We love each other.* (BETTY hangs up.) *Atilah! Come here. You've got to help us all get ready to go and hear your father speak—come on now!*

(Interior. Day. MALCOLM, naked in the shower, letting the water roll over him.

Under the sound of the water, we hear voices.)

LOUISE'S VOICE *Go stand in the sun and get some color, boy.*

SHORTY'S VOICE *That's Homeboy. From Detroit.—Hold still now. This shit can burn a hole in your head.*

LUTHER'S VOICE *—the man who raped your mother and murdered your father! And you got the nerve to call yourself a man!*

SIDNEY'S VOICE *When you get us out of prison.*

(The side-view mirror: the streets of Harlem.

We stop before the Audubon Ballroom.

MALCOLM nervously wipes his glasses, puts them on, enters the hall.

The anteroom of the Audubon.

MALCOLM, BENJAMIN, and a YOUNG LADY are sitting perfectly still.

The hall, slowly filling with people. There is no center aisle. There are no policemen.

BETTY and the CHILDREN enter, sitting quite far in the back.

The Anteroom.)

MALCOLM *Where is Reverend What-his-name?*

YOUNG LADY *Brother Malcolm, I'm not sure he's going to be able to make it. He did warn us that he had another engagement. And I think we'd better start. Brother Benjamin—will you introduce Brother Malcolm?*

MALCOLM *You know better than to ask him something like that in front of me!*

YOUNG LADY *Brother Malcolm—I'm sorry—I didn't think—*

MALCOLM *I'm sorry. I didn't think.*

BROTHER BENJAMIN *I'd be happy and I'd be honored to introduce you, Brother Malcolm, if you've got no objections.*

MALCOLM *Brother Benjamin—I don't know what's wrong with me today. I'd be happy and honored if you would introduce me.*

YOUNG LADY *Then we'd better start. The house is full.*

(BENJAMIN X exits. We hear the roar of applause that greets him.

MALCOLM: pacing.)

MALCOLM   *How long will he speak?*

YOUNG LADY   *Oh, not more than half an hour.*

(MALCOLM glances at his watch: continues pacing.
The YOUNG LADY: watching MALCOLM.
Close-up: MALCOLM's wristwatch, as he paces.
Close-up: MALCOLM: as BENJAMIN X ends his introduction.)

VOICE OF BENJAMIN X OVER   *—and now, without further remarks, I present to you one who is willing to put himself on the line for you, a man who would give his life for you. I want you to hear, listen, understand—one who is a Trojan for the black man— Mr. Malcolm X!*

(Close-up: a weary MALCOLM, as he hears the roar of applause.

MALCOLM pauses at the door, and then turns back to the YOUNG LADY.)

MALCOLM   *I'm sorry. You'll have to forgive me for raising my voice to you—I'm just about at my wits' end.*

YOUNG LADY   *Please don't mention it. I understand.*

MALCOLM   *I wonder if anybody* really *understands.*

(He walks onto the stage, smiling and shaking hands with BENJAMIN X, who goes into the anteroom.
Close-up: BETTY, as MALCOLM comes on stage.)

MALCOLM   *As-Salaam-Alaikum, Brothers and Sisters!*

VOICES   *Wa-Alaikum-Salaam!*

(Close-up: MALCOLM, reacting to a tremendous confusion at the rear of the hall.)

MAN'S VOICE OVER   *Get your hand out of my pocket!*

MALCOLM   *Hold it! Hold it, Brothers! Don't get excited. Let's cool it, Brothers!*

(Then the volley hits him.
From MALCOLM's point of view:
Black men, standing, firing, running.
Horrified faces, now frozen, now fluid.
The lights above him.
MALCOLM throws up both hands, then grabs his chest and falls backward.
We hear cries and screams and more firing but we

remain hypnotized by the space which MALCOLM has deserted.

Then, the pregnant BETTY screams, and comes into view, and falls over the body of her husband.

Morning. The Temple in Harlem, from which MALCOLM will be taken to be buried.

People slowly lining up before this Temple, many of them white, all silent.

SHORTY takes his place in the line.

In the Temple: BETTY, utterly still.

Dusk. A light rain is falling in the cemetery.

Close-up: the coffin, with the inscription, *El Haji Malik El Shabazz, May 1925–February 21, 1965.*

Some of MALCOLM's followers drop earth on the tomb, and then pick up shovels and prepare to fill the hole.

We leave them at this labor, and travel through the streets of Harlem in the light rain, as night is falling.

LAURA, walking very slowly.)

MALCOLM'S VOICE OVER   *And if I can die, having brought any light, having helped expose the racist cancer that is malignant in the body of America— all of the credit is due to Allah. Only the mistakes have been mine.*

BETTY'S VOICE OVER   *You are present when you are away.*

268